AF290978

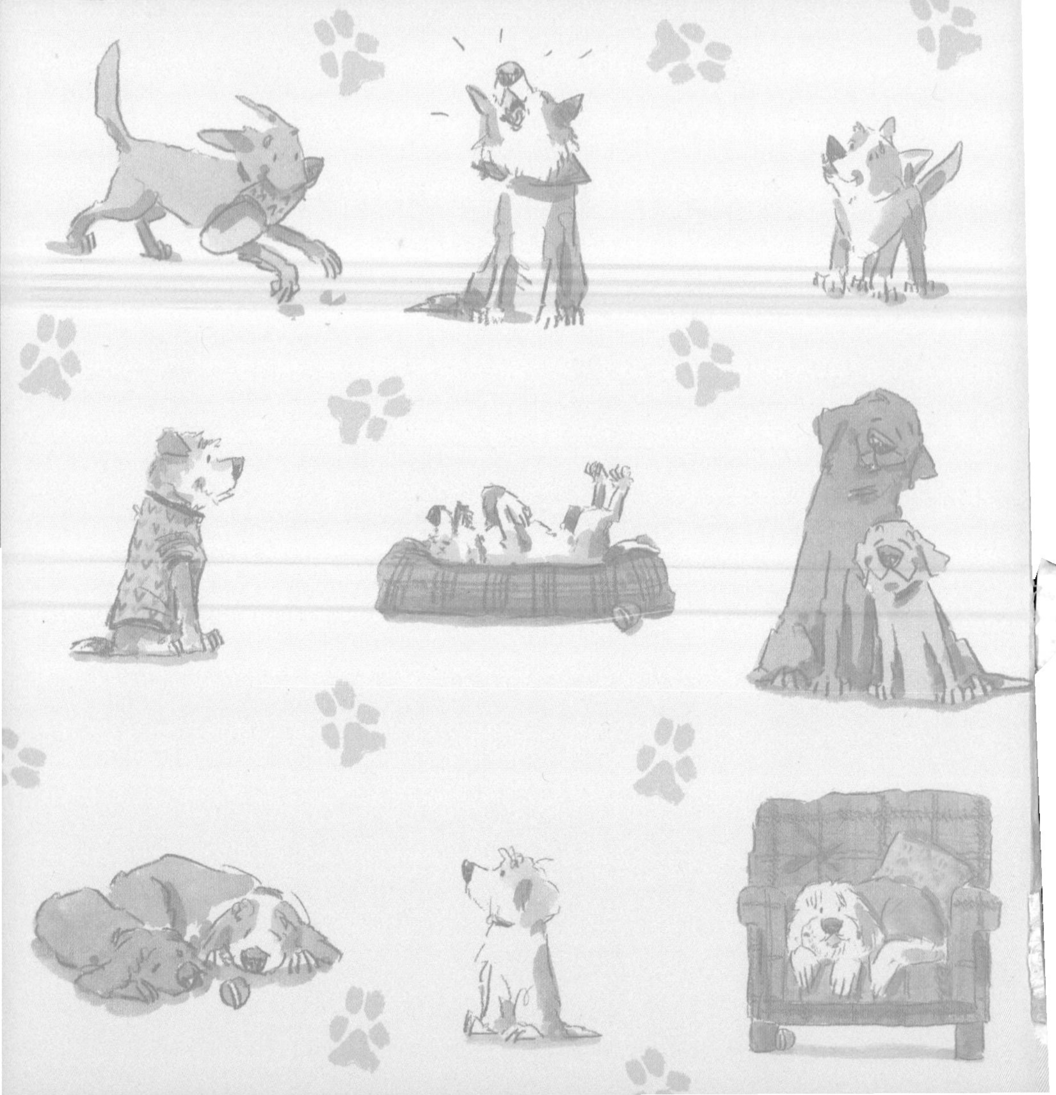

IT'S A TOUGH JOB BEING A DOG

Life through a dog's eyes

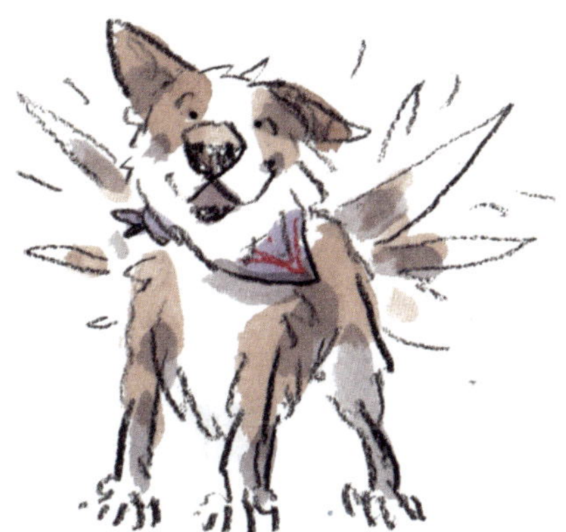

IAIN WELCH

HarperCollins*Publishers*

HarperCollins*Publishers*
1 London Bridge Street
London SE1 9GF

www.harpercollins.co.uk

HarperCollins*Publishers*
Macken House, 39/40 Mayor Street Upper
Dublin 1, D01 C9W8, Ireland

First published by HarperCollins*Publishers* 2026

1 3 5 7 9 10 8 6 4 2

A catalogue record of this book is available from the British Library

HB ISBN 978-0-00-879538-2

Printed and bound at PNB, Latvia

Work

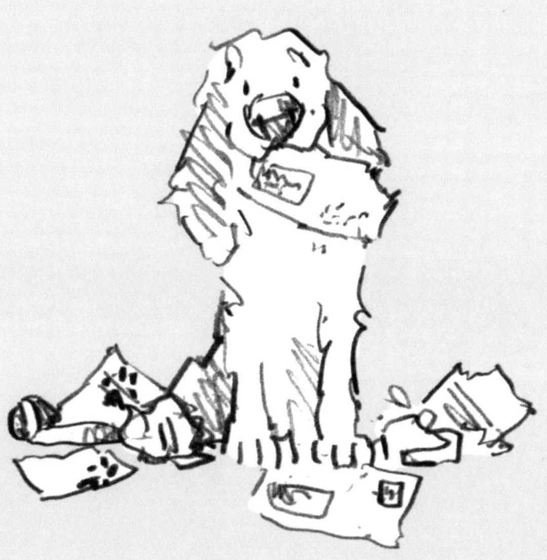

I throw myself into my
work every day.

I put all of my
dogginess into it.

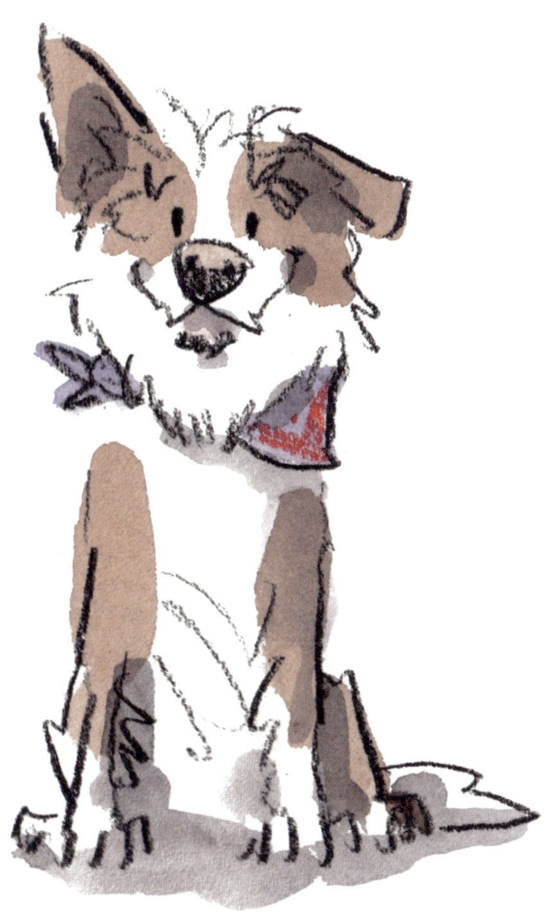

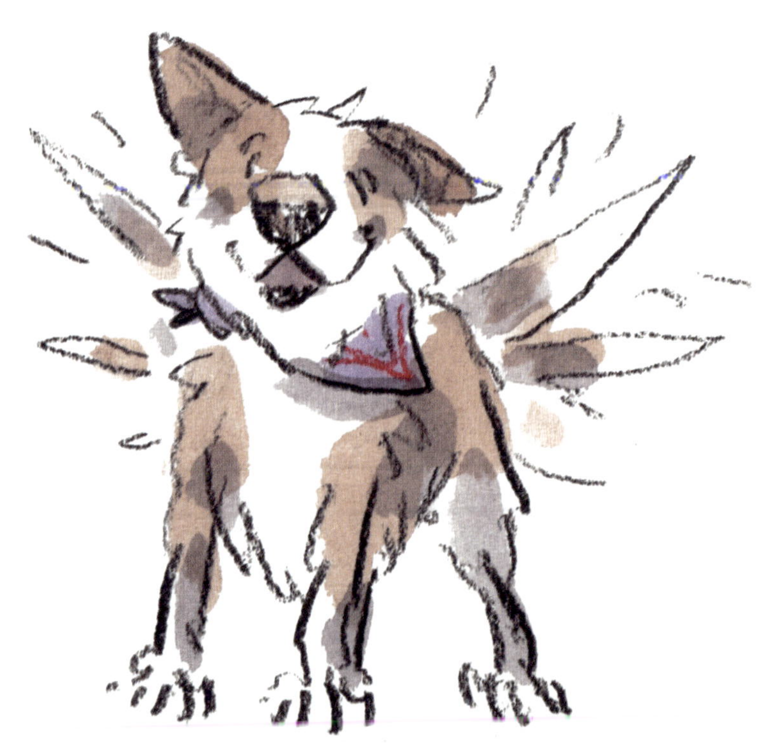

I wag the biggest,

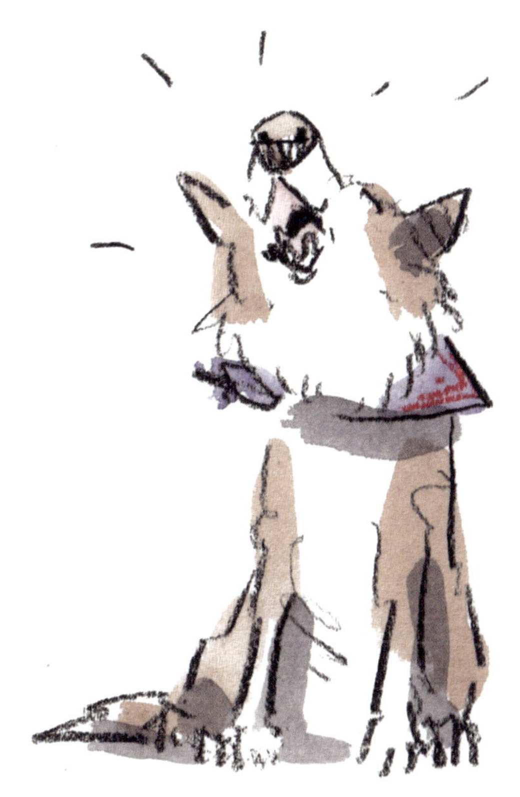

bark the loudest,

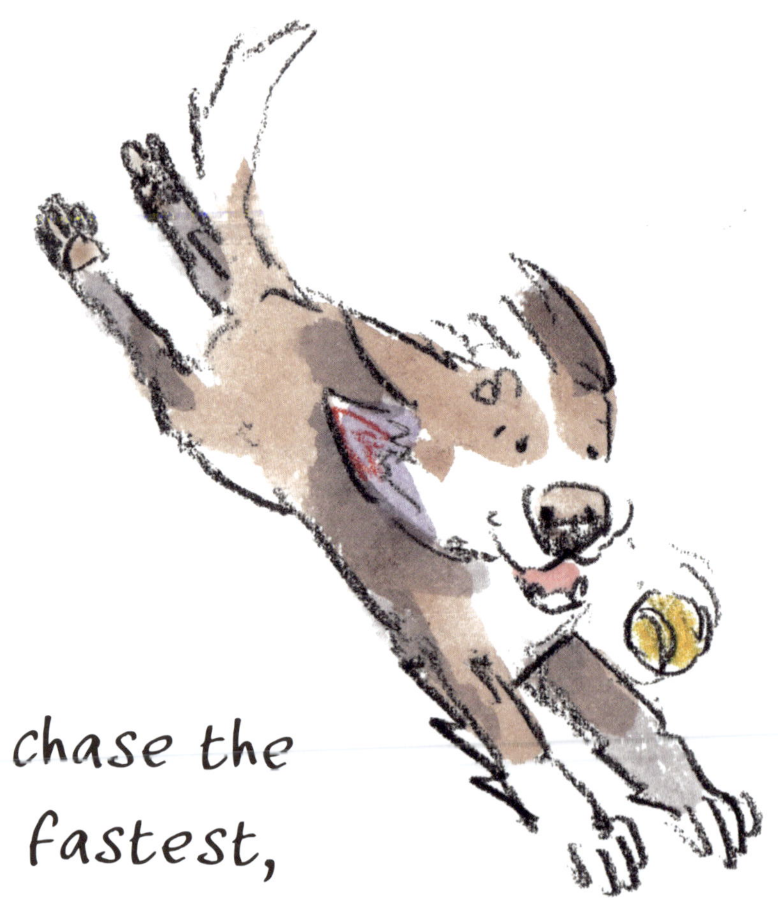

chase the
fastest,

and play the bestest that
I possibly can.

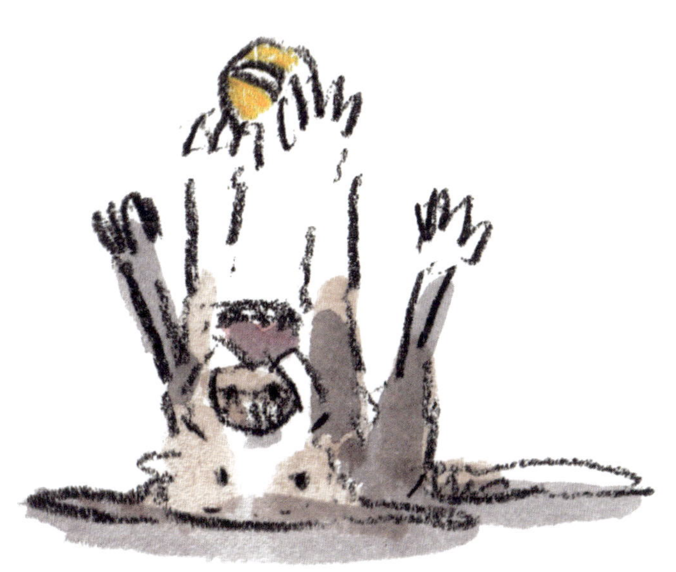

I am a very
hard-working dog...
and I think that I
deserve a treat.

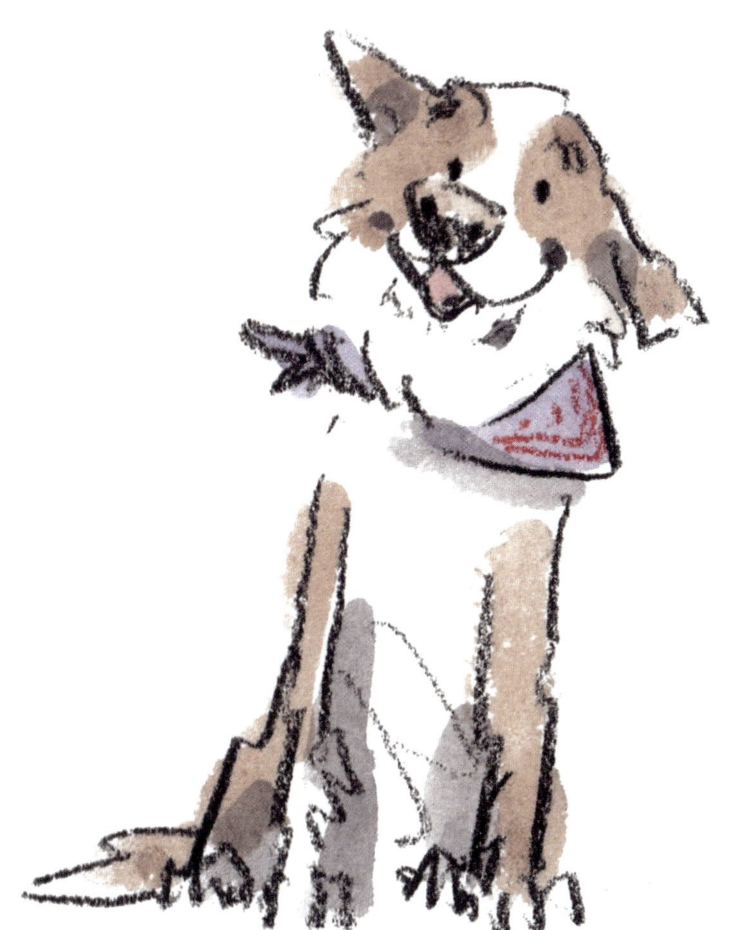

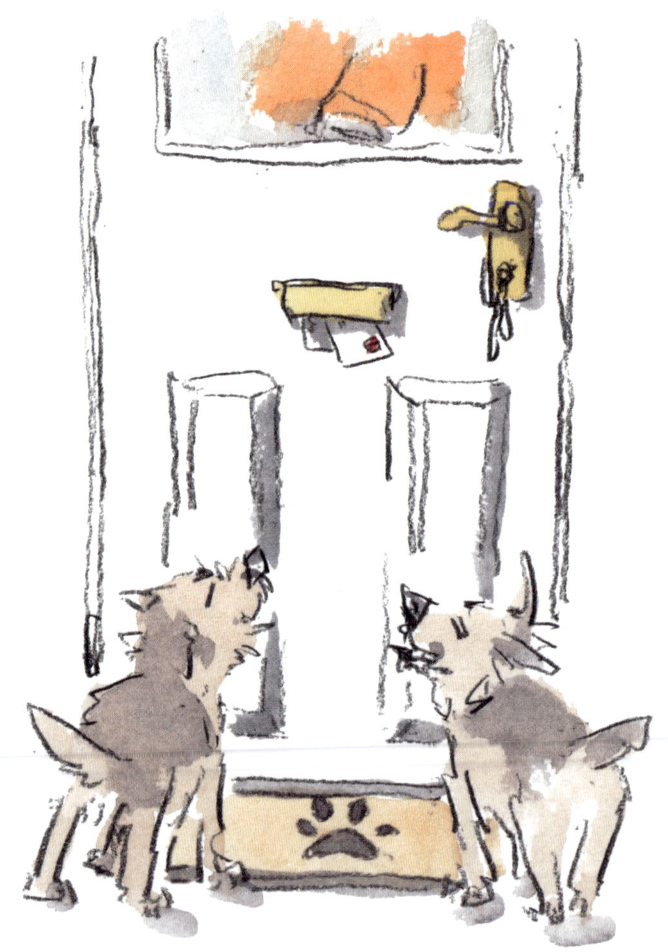

Do you know, he has
never once offered to
bark at the postie for
us so that we can have
a day off.

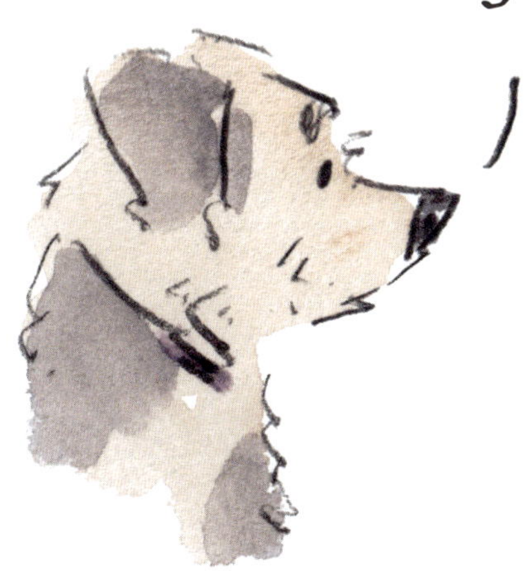

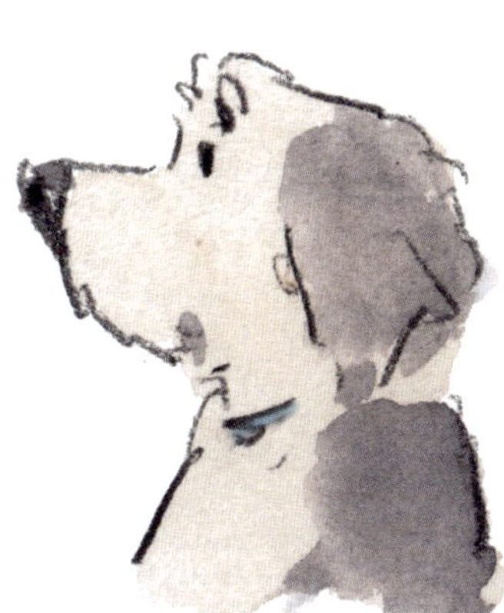

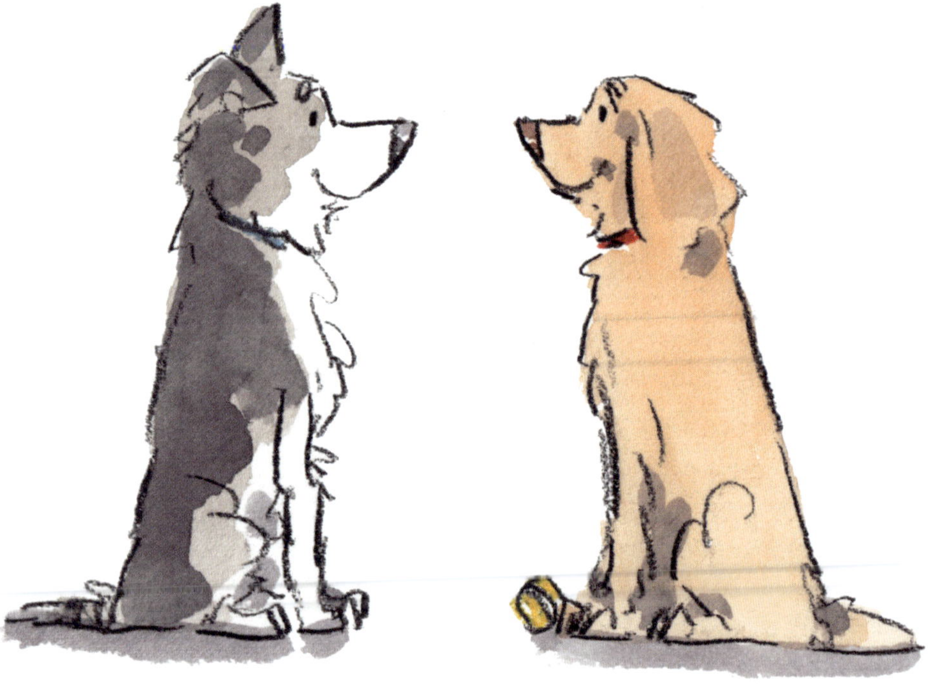

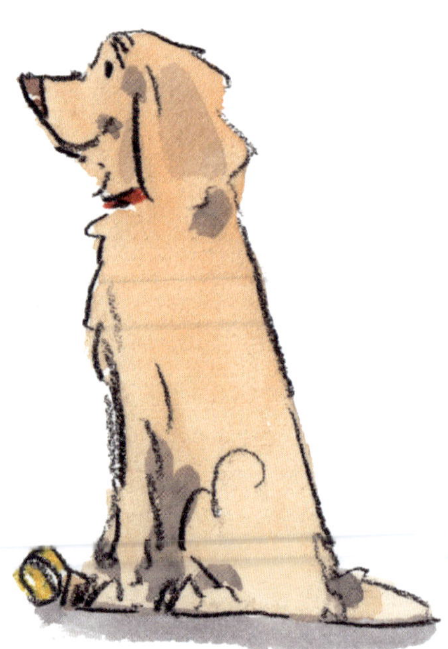

My people make me
work around the
house all of the time.

I have to help with the laundry,

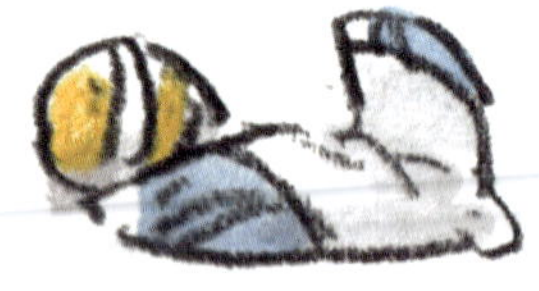

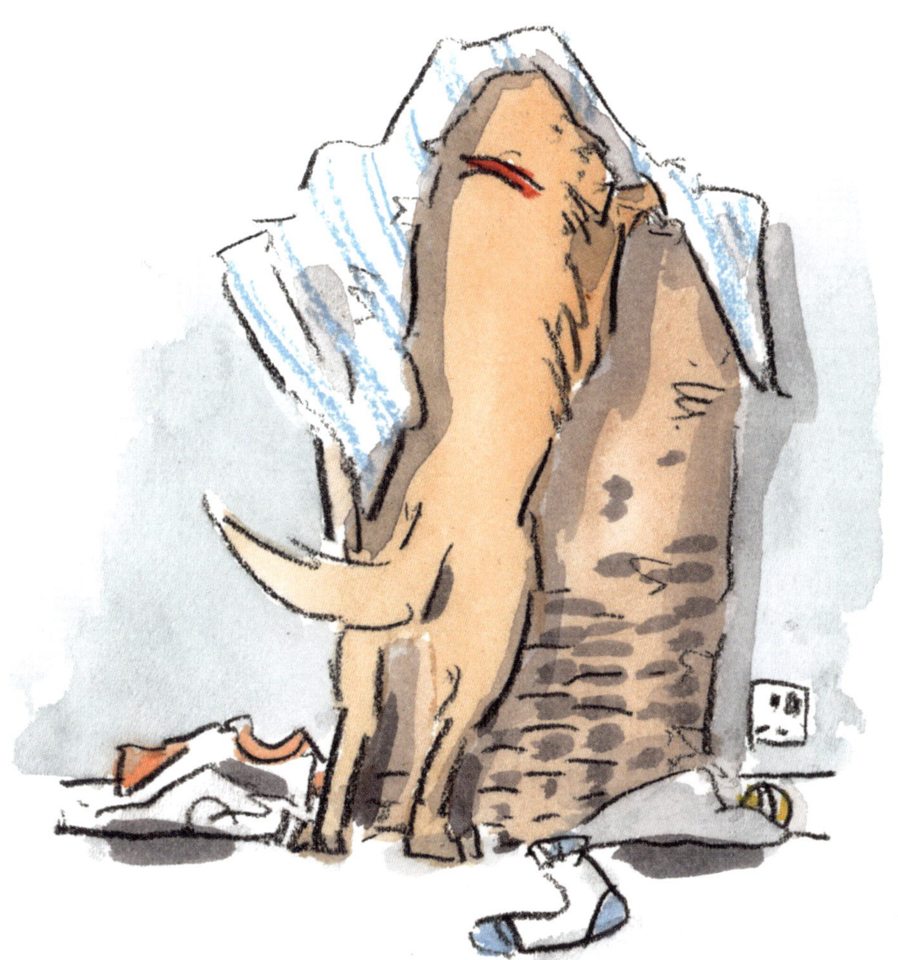

I have to
work in the
garden,

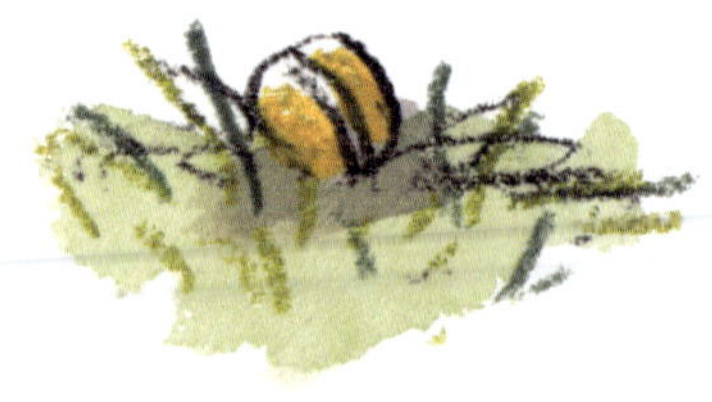

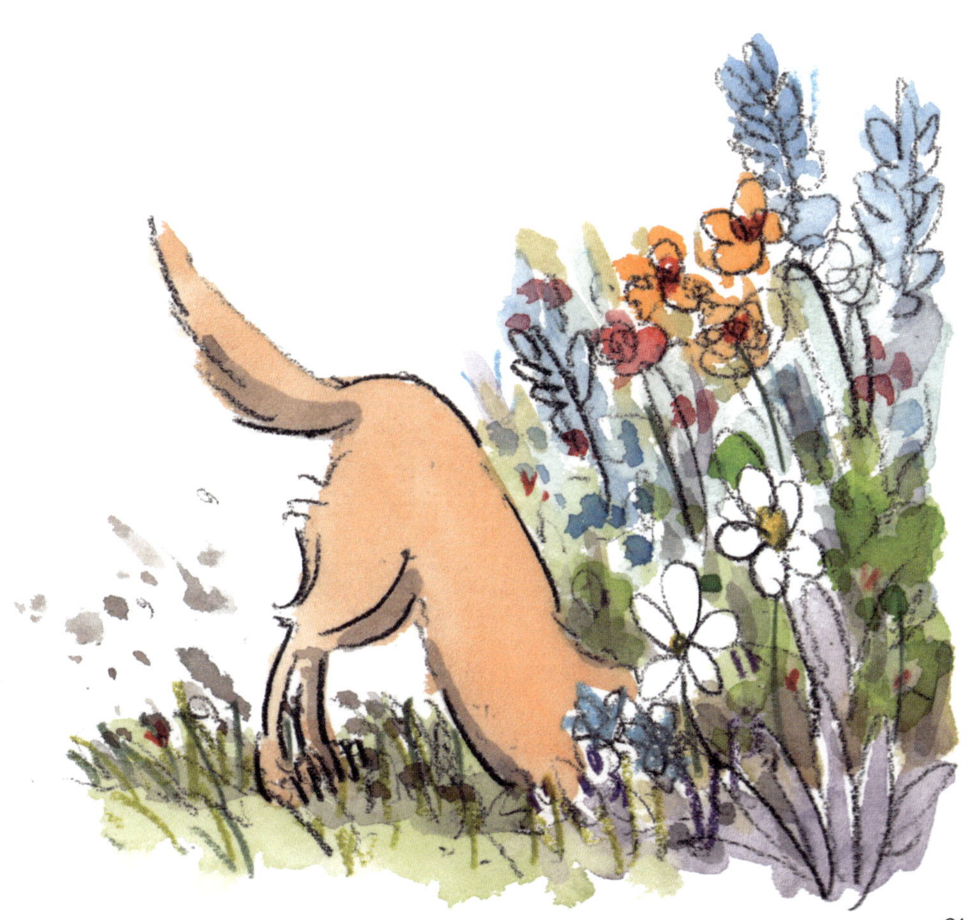

I work
hard in the
office,

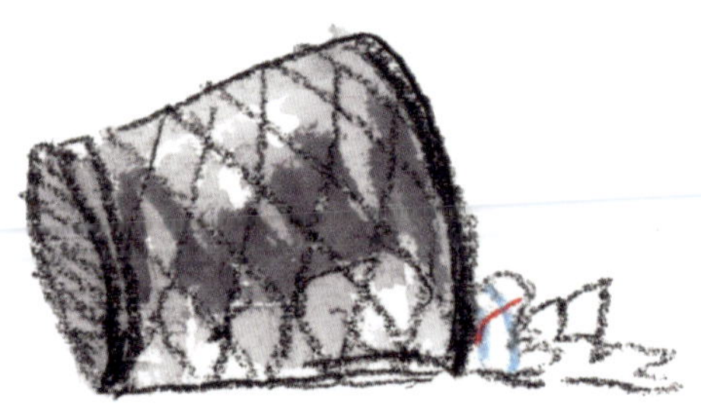

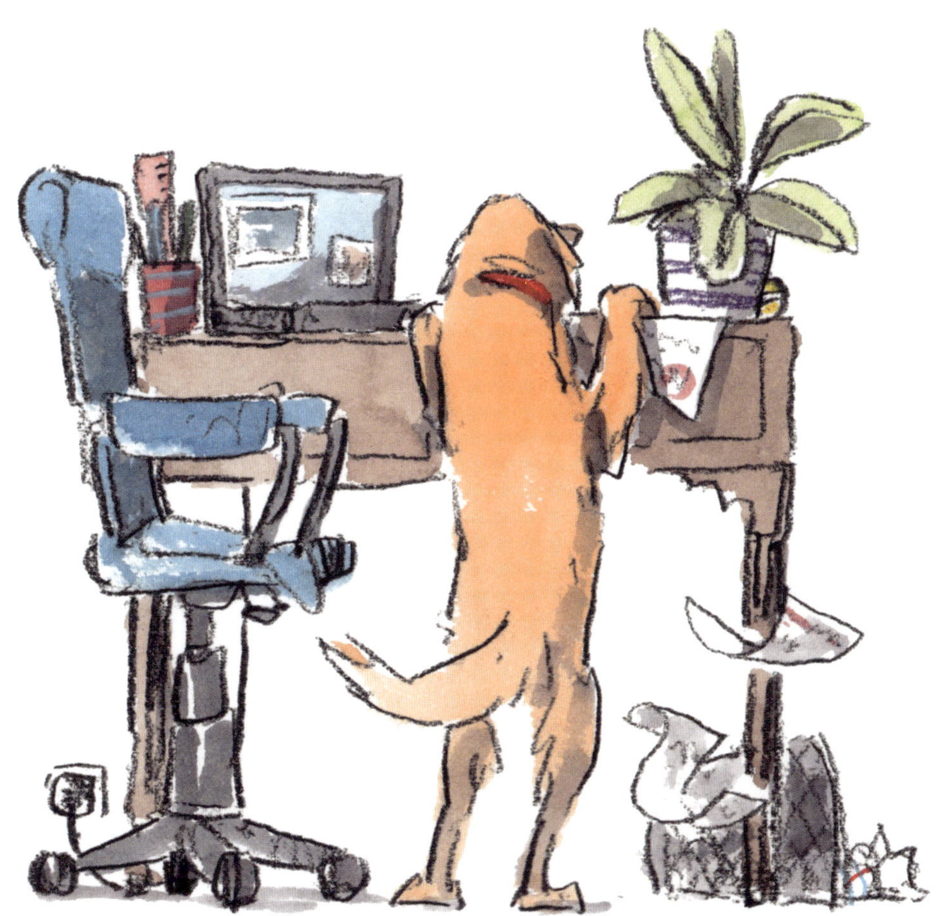

and I work
even harder
in the kitchen.

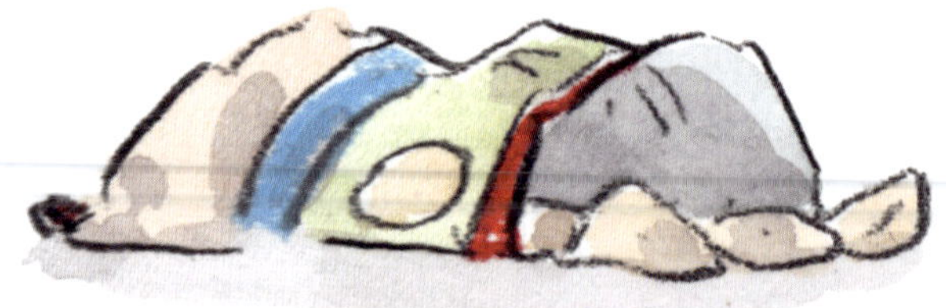

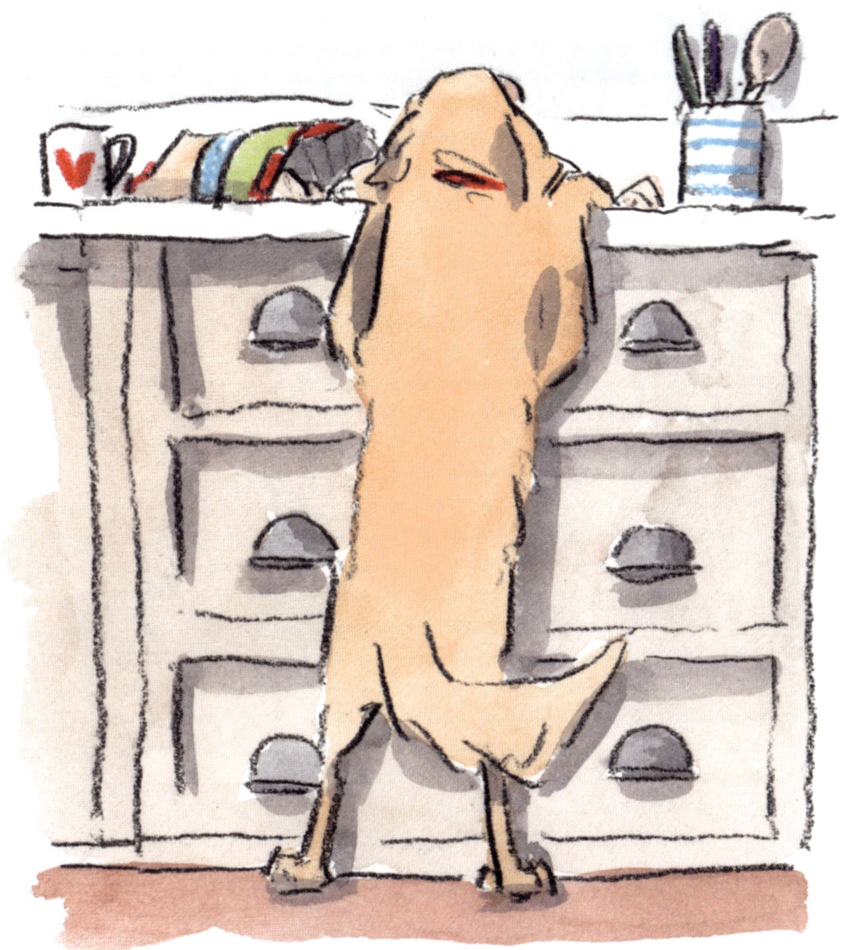

It's a lot of
effort but I think
that they are
worth it.

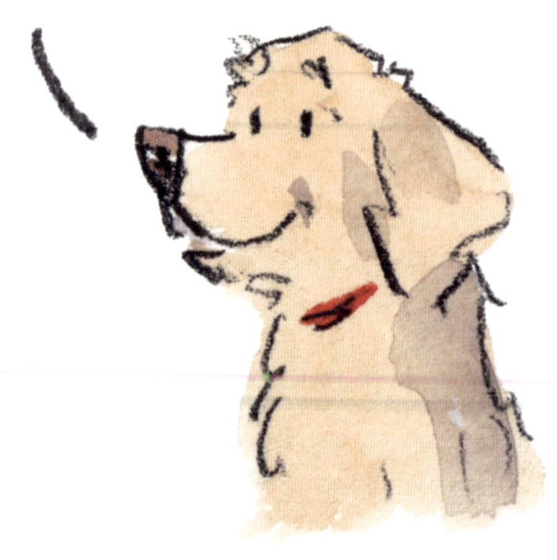

My plan is to get all of my work done on Monday so that I can have the rest of the week off.

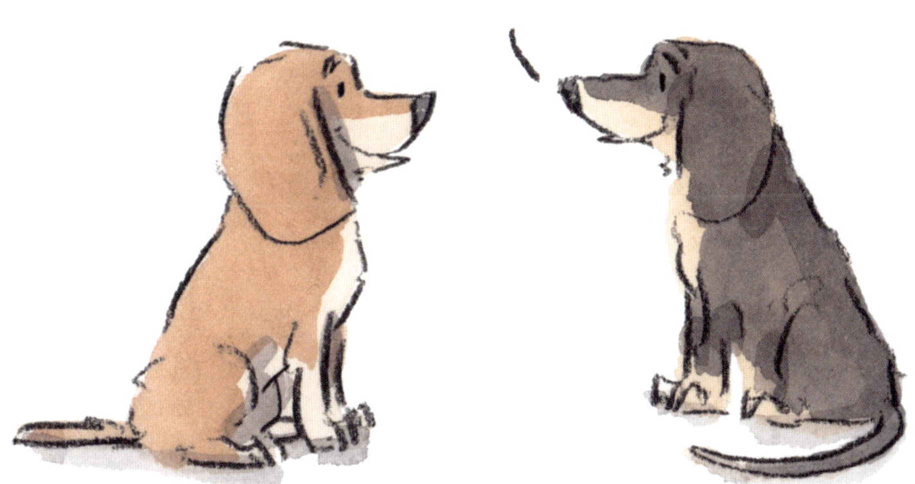

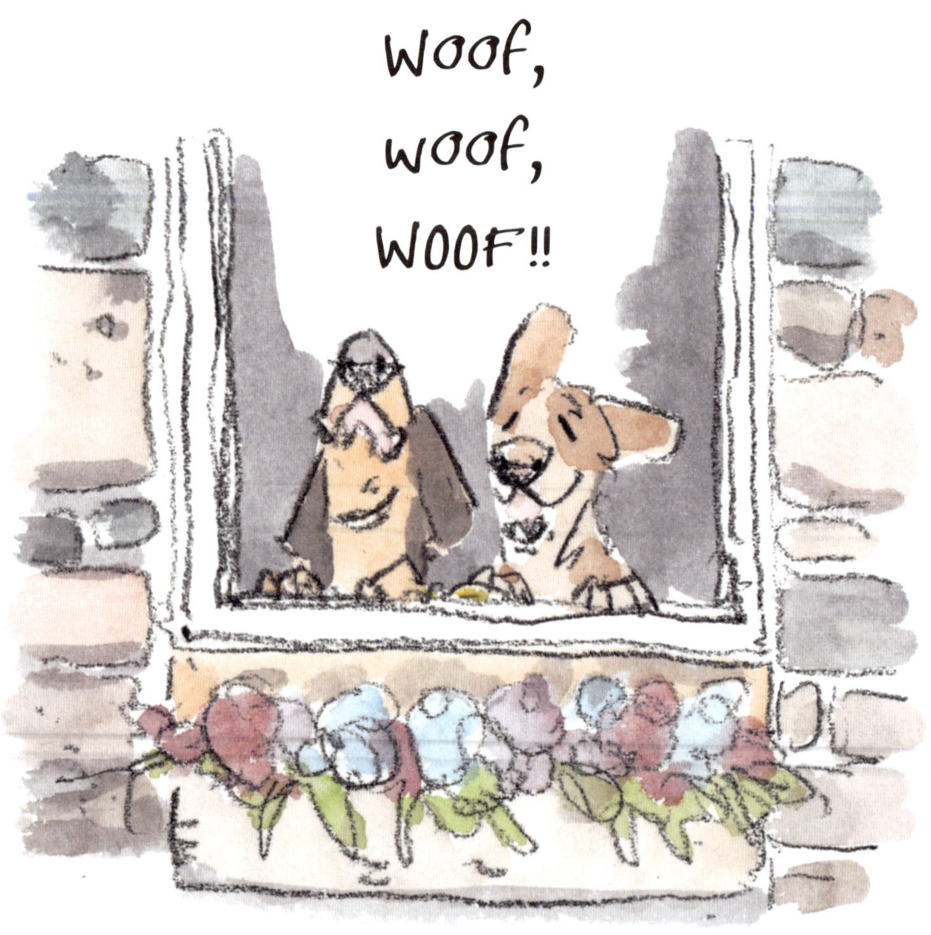

28

It is our solemn duty
to make sure that
everyone is properly
barked at.

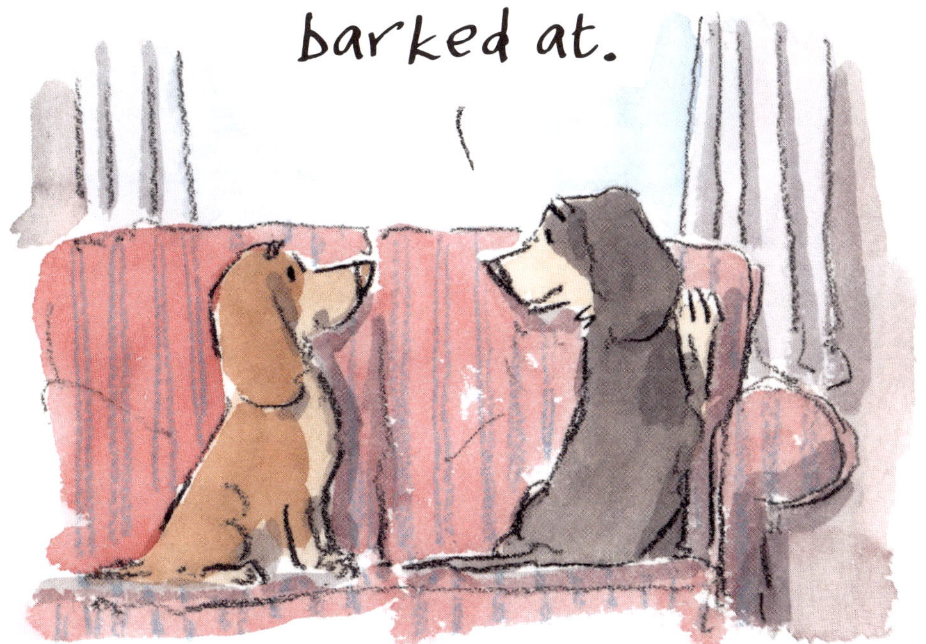

And so I told him...

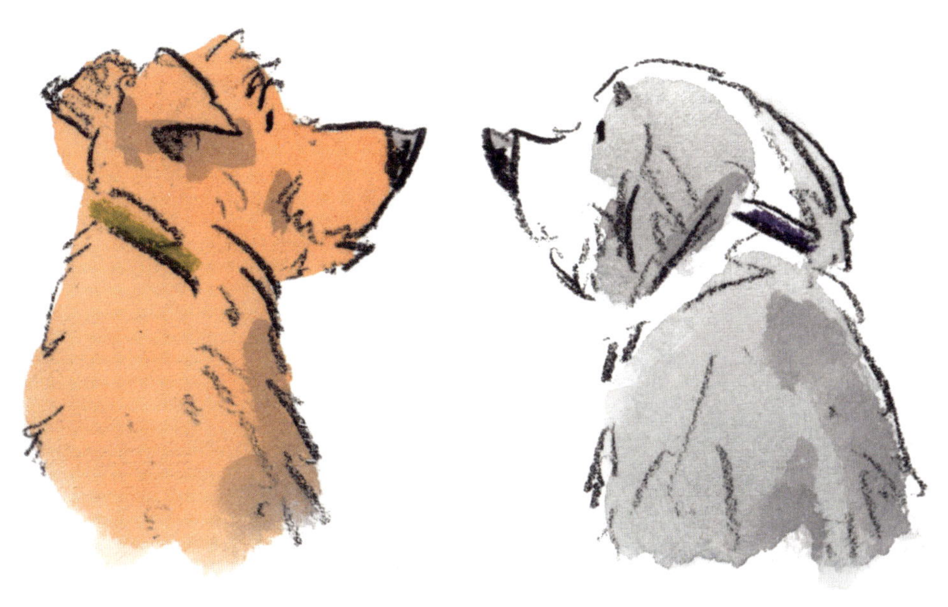

...on the walks,
I'll do all of the hard
work...

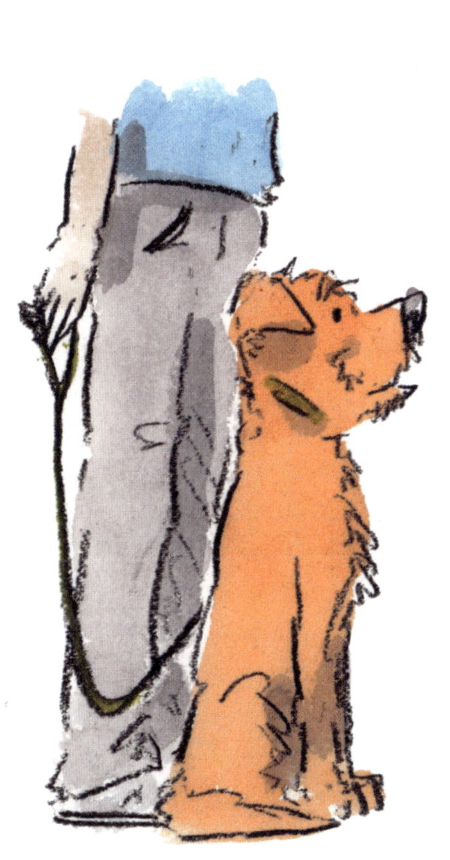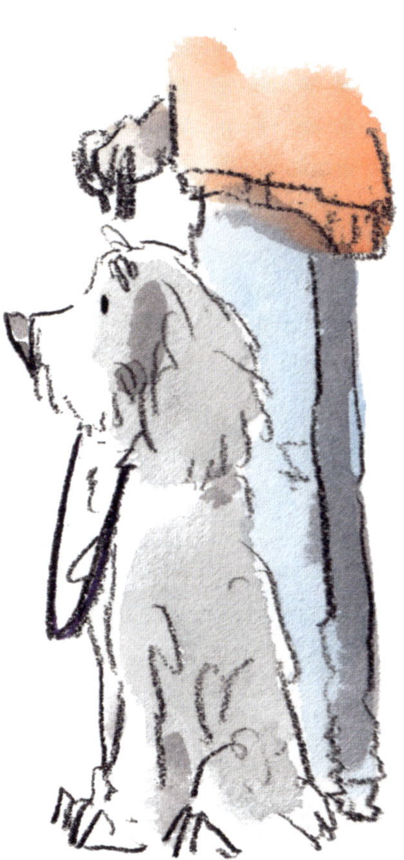

...I'll do all of the chasing of the ball and then the bringing back of the ball....

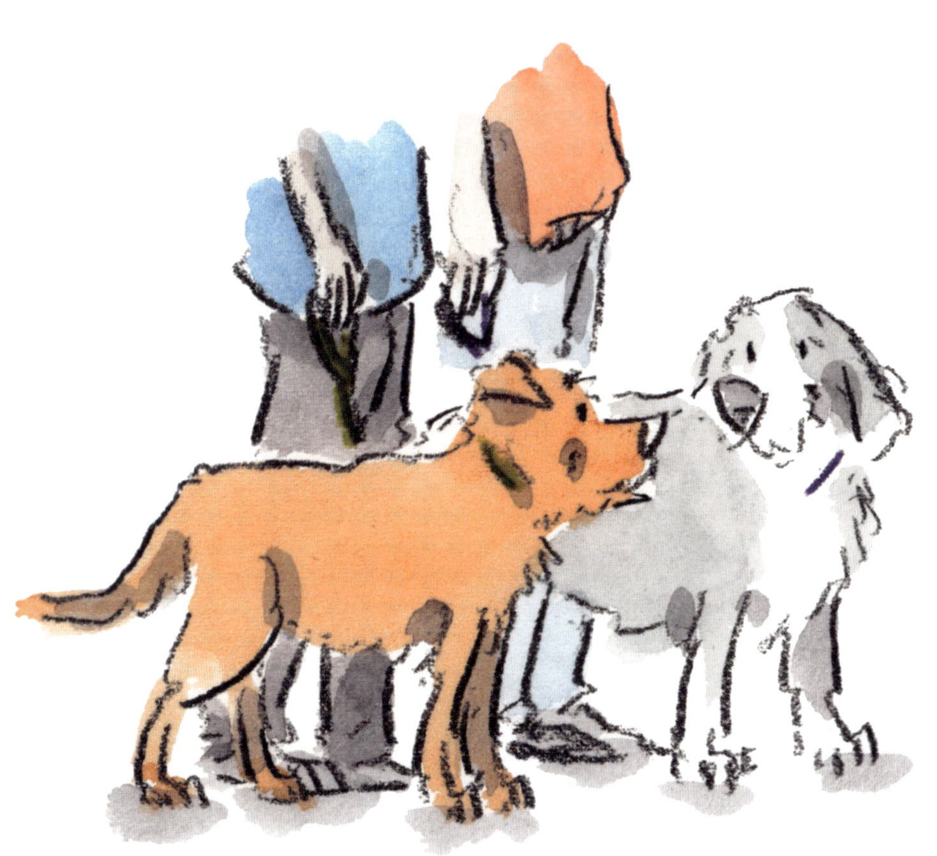

...I'll do all of the sniffing things and then the peeing on things...

...all he needs to do is
to bring the snacks.

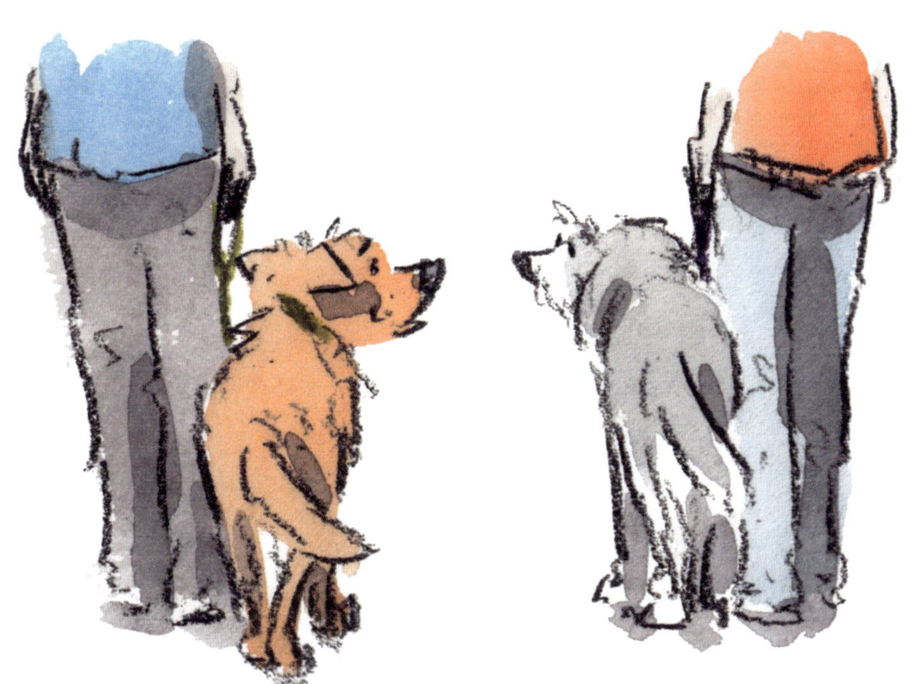

That sounds like
a really good deal
to me.

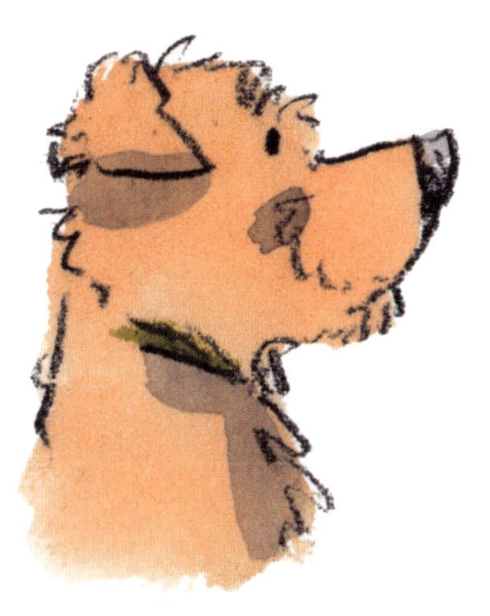 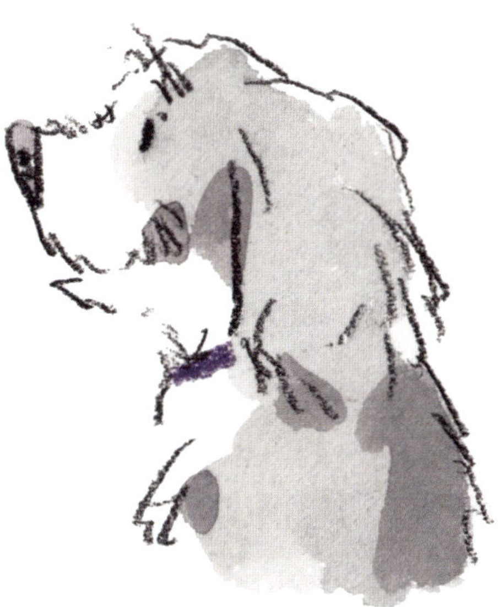

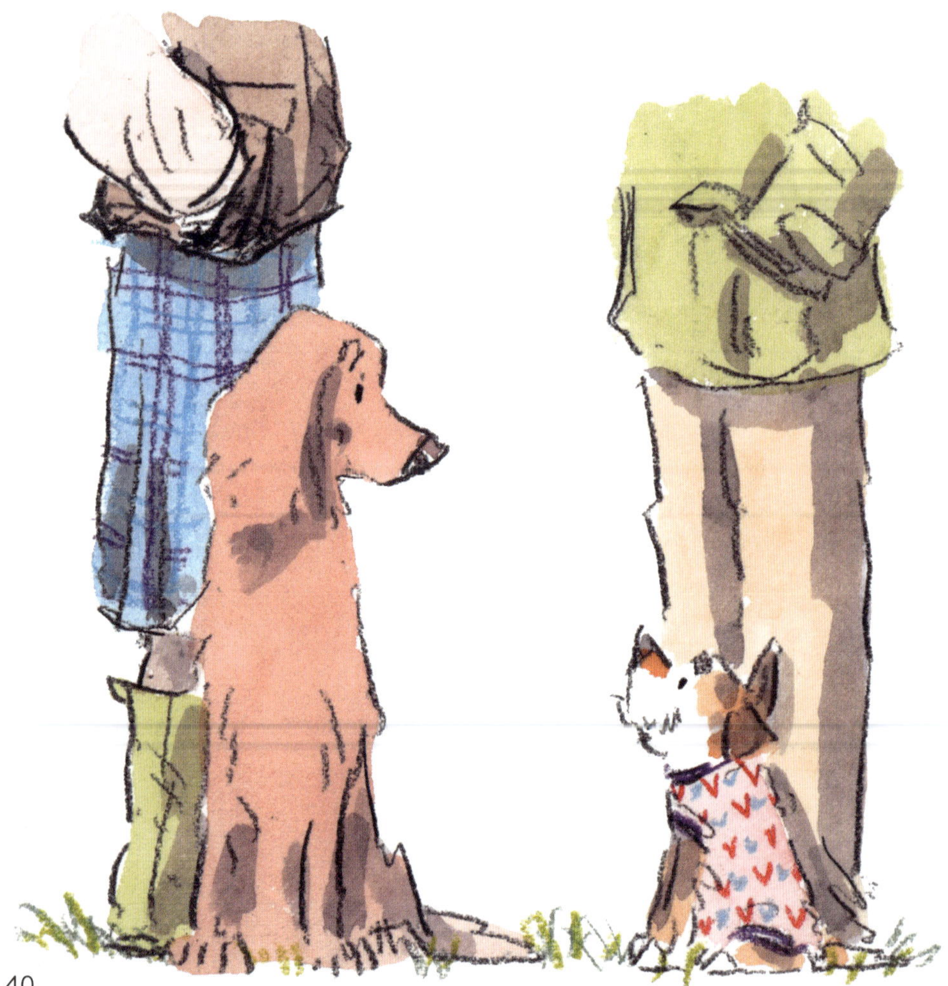

My job on walks is to
keep him safe.

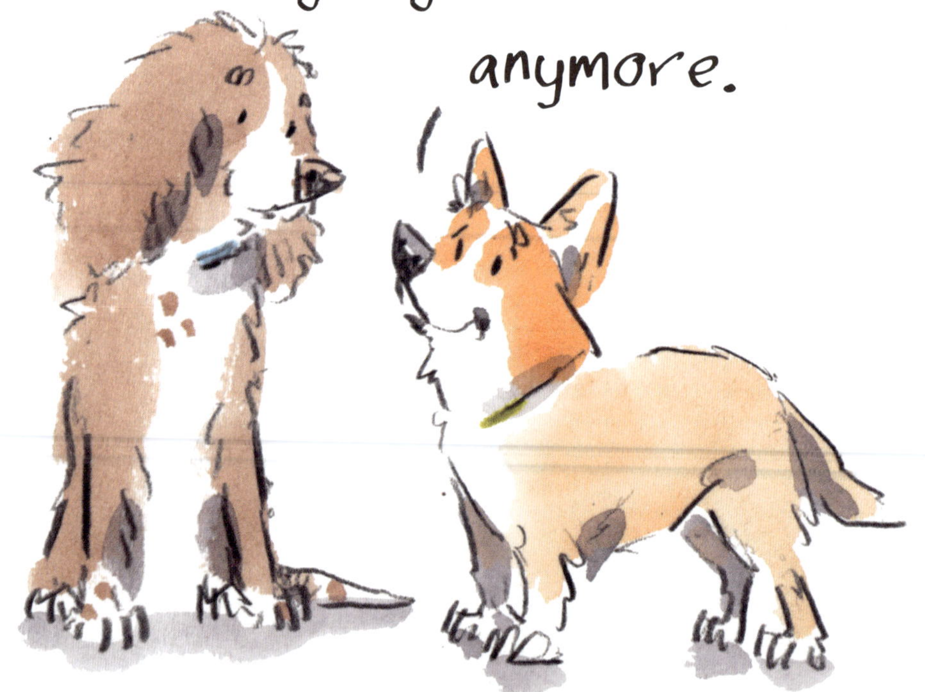

I'm overworked
and underpaid. I'm not
going to stand for it
anymore.

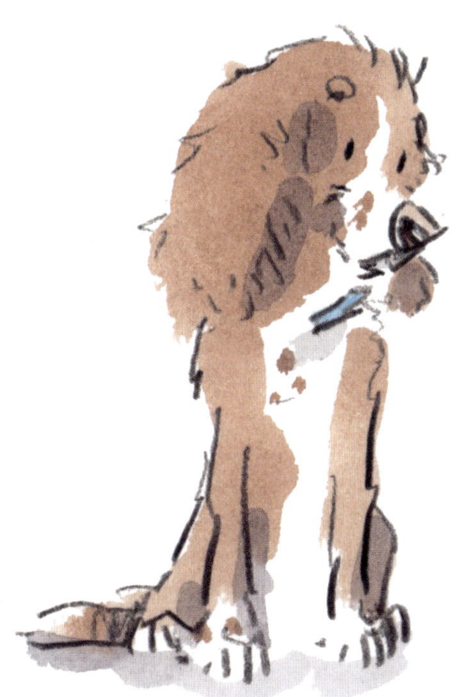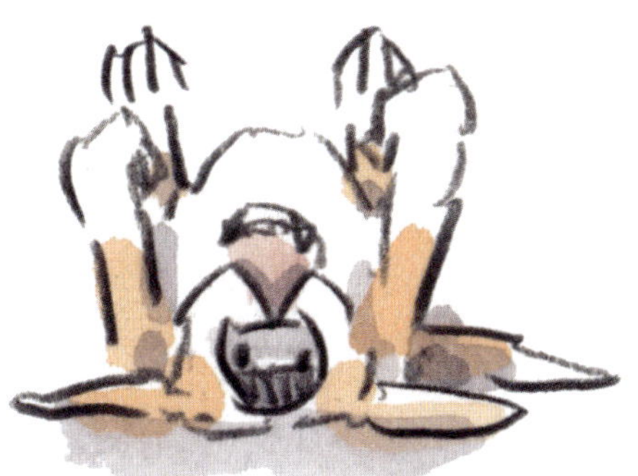

There,
that's better.

Play

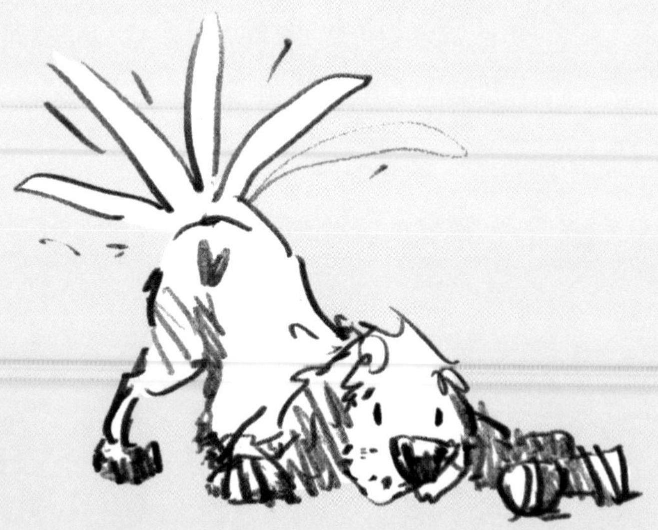

Would you mind, awfully, throwing my ball for me, please?

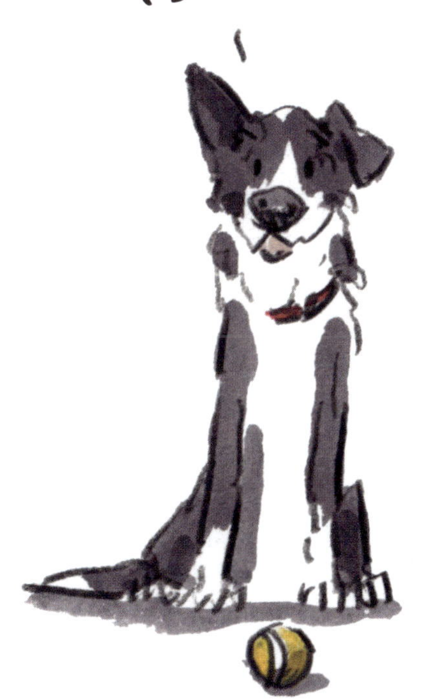

Our job is to fill every
day with as much fun and
play as we can.

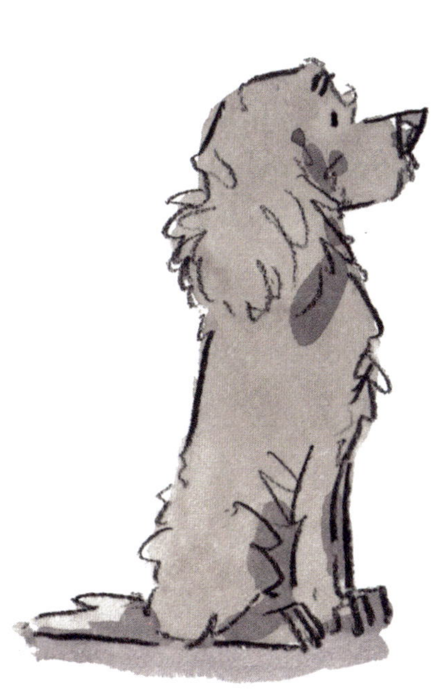
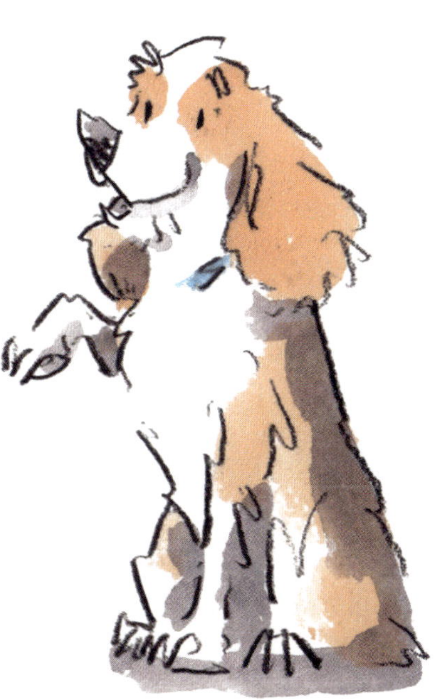

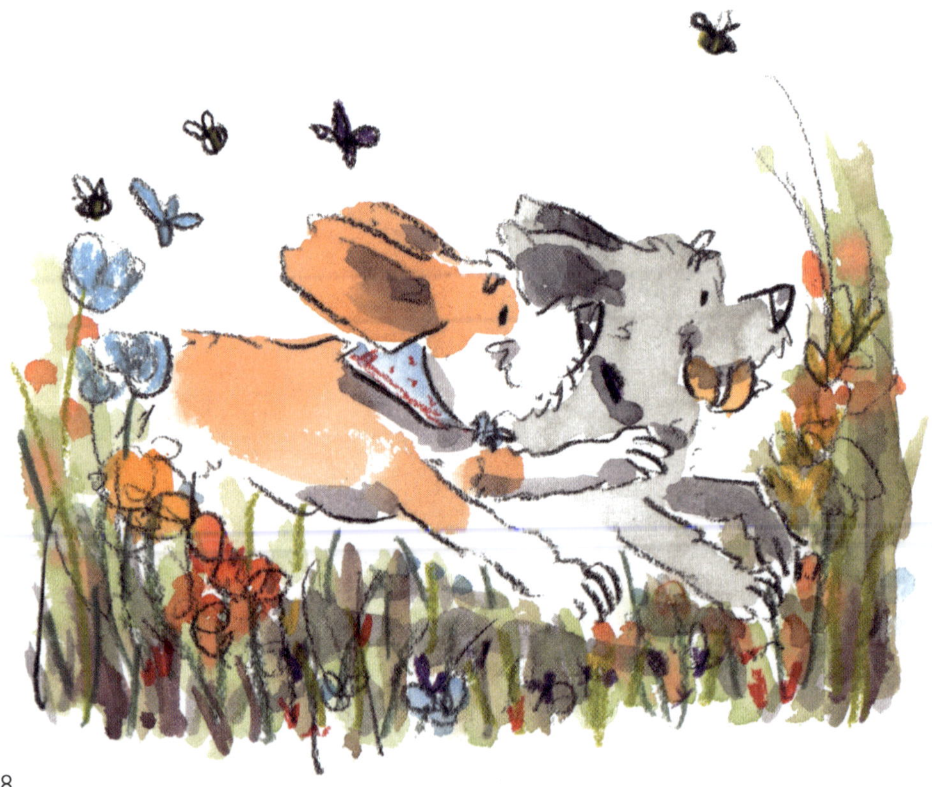

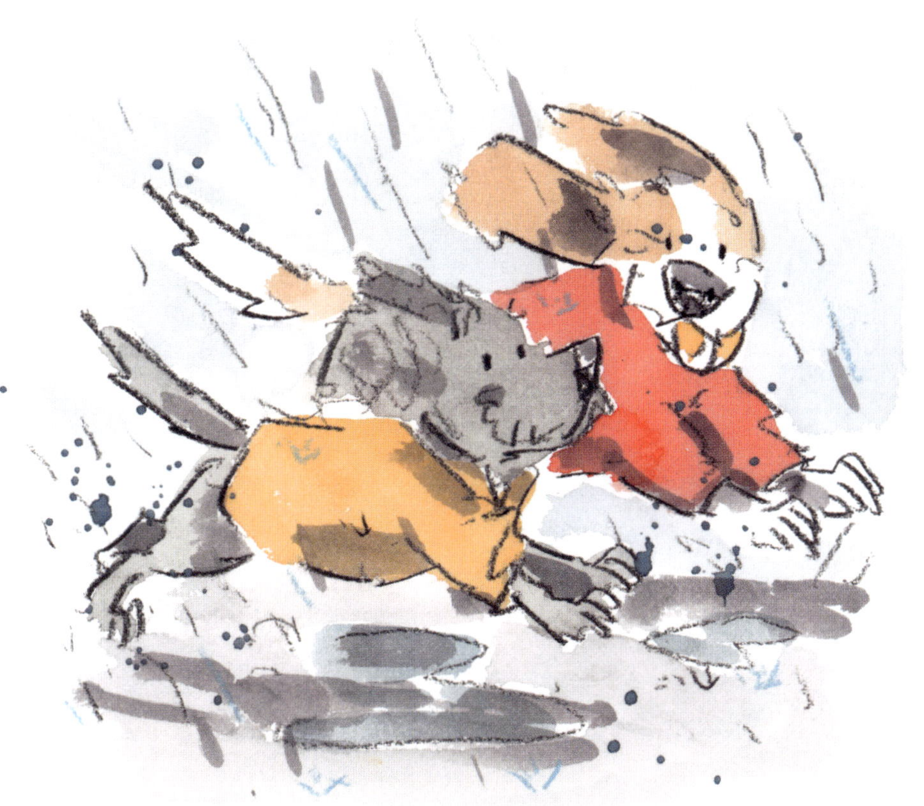

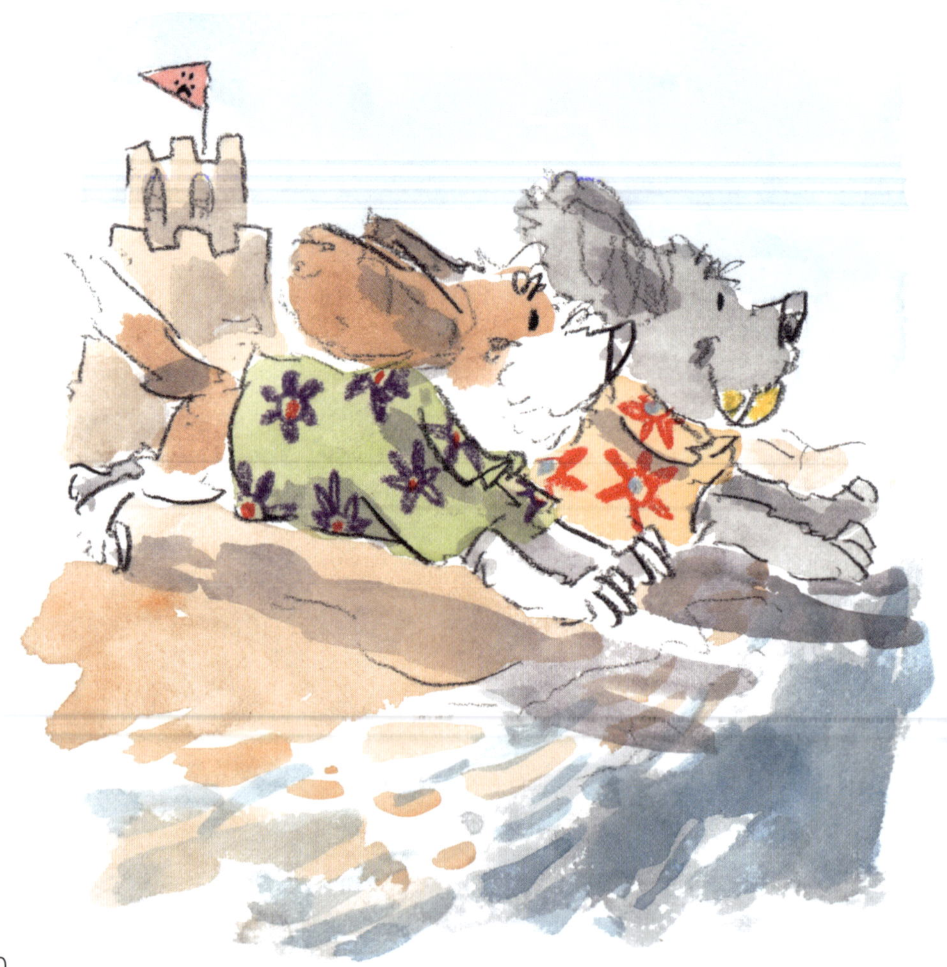

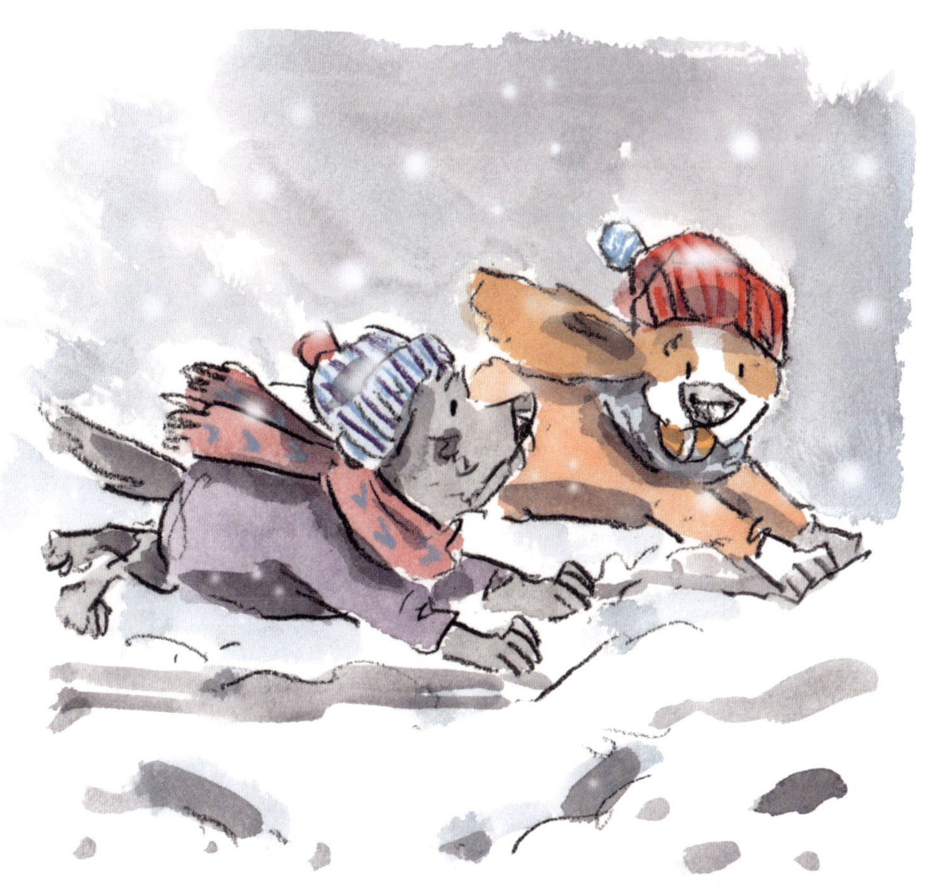

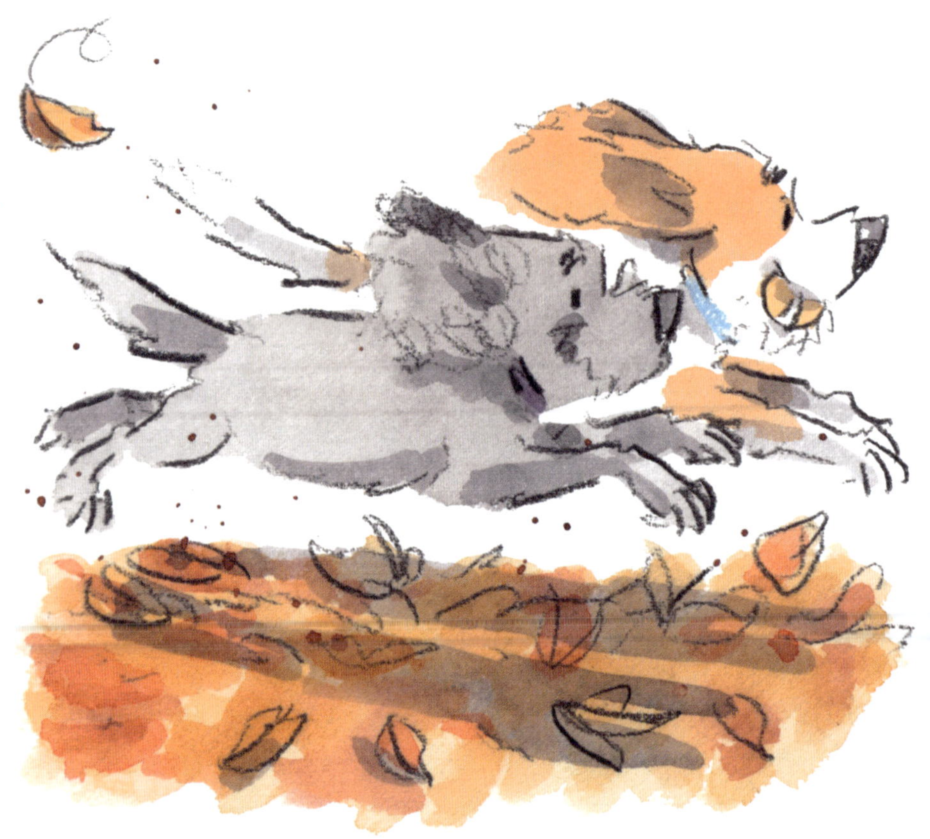

And then, after a day
of fun and play,

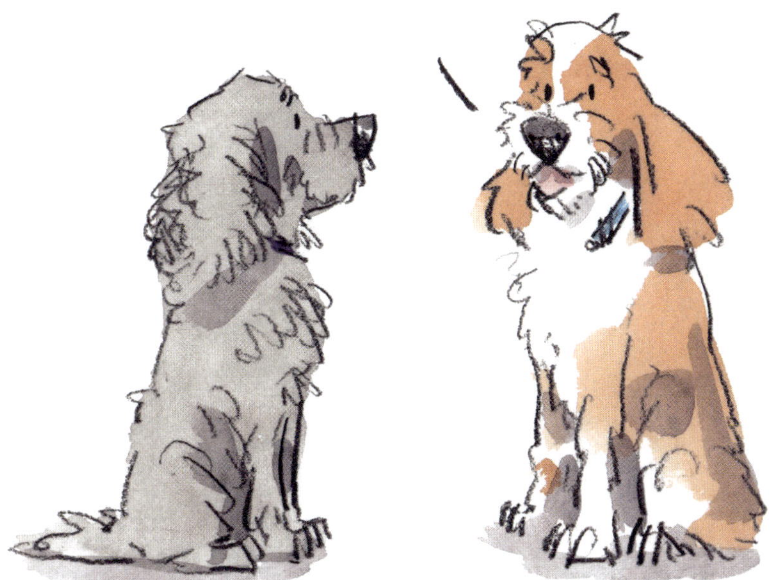

we can have a
lovely sleep and
dream about
tomorrow.

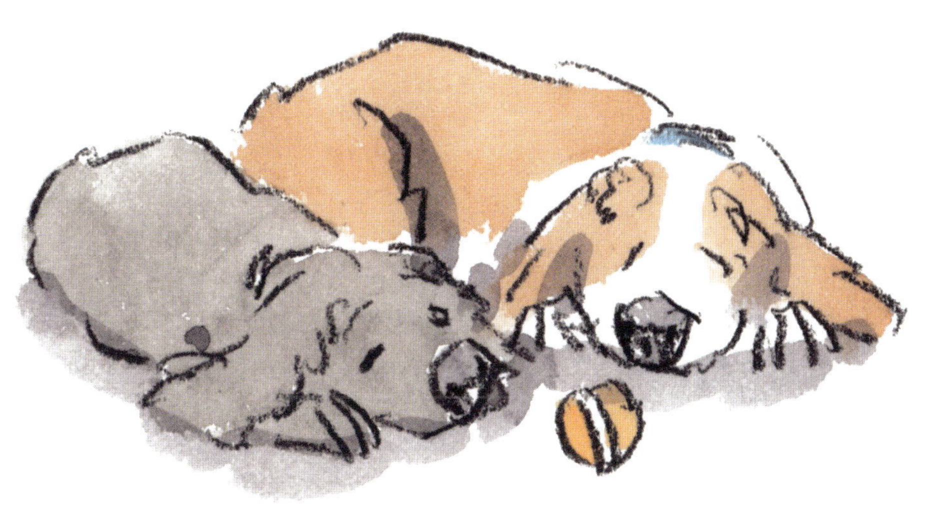

Pup, your job is to provide them with one hundred percent of their recommended daily amount of mischief.

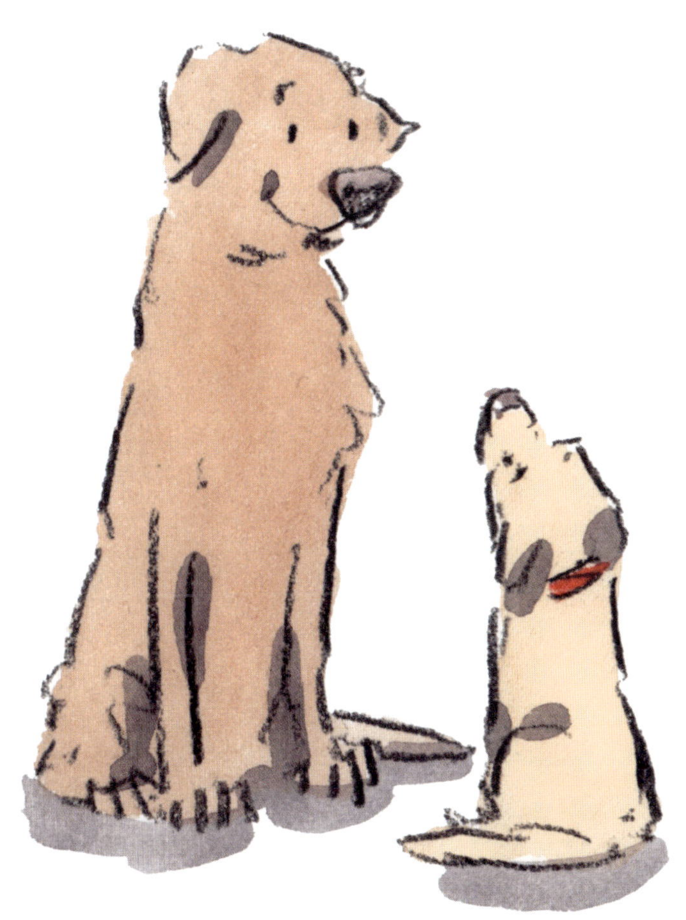

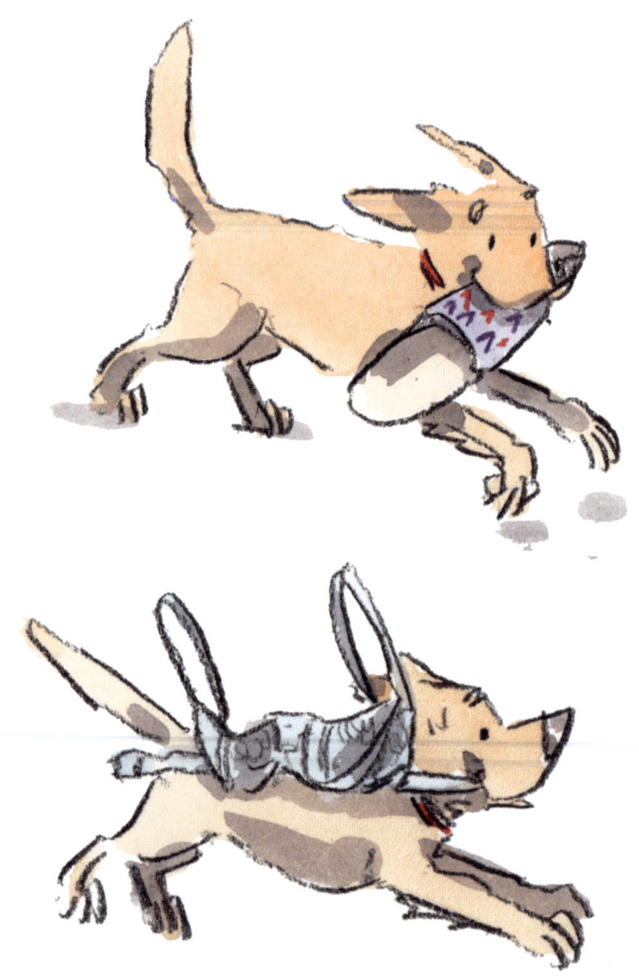

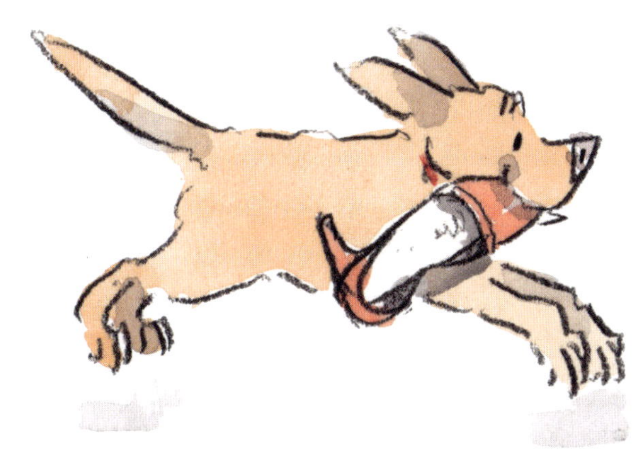

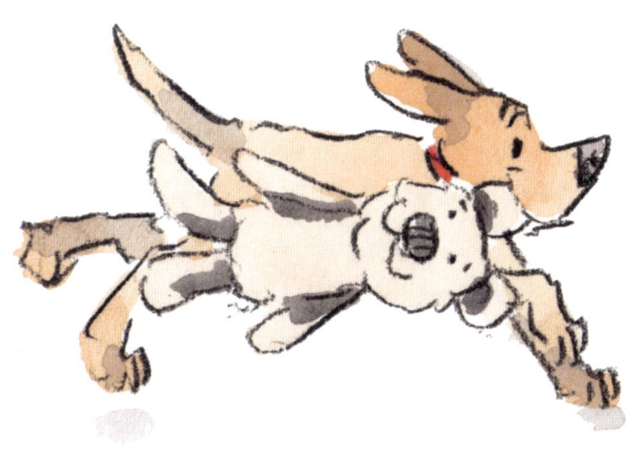

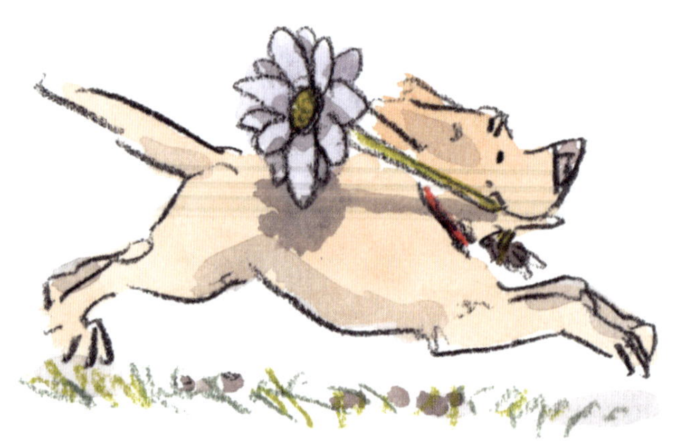

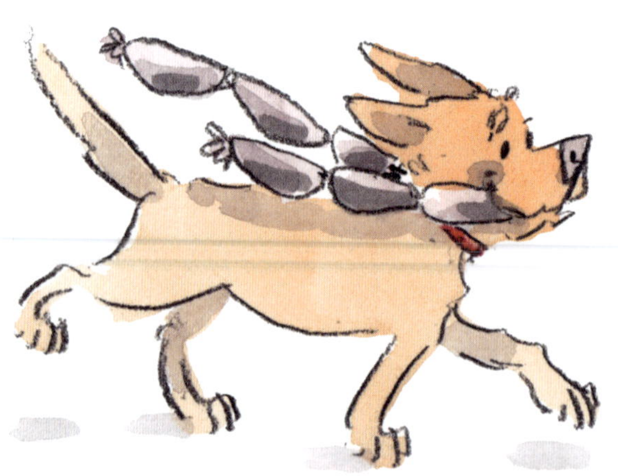

Excellent work, pup.

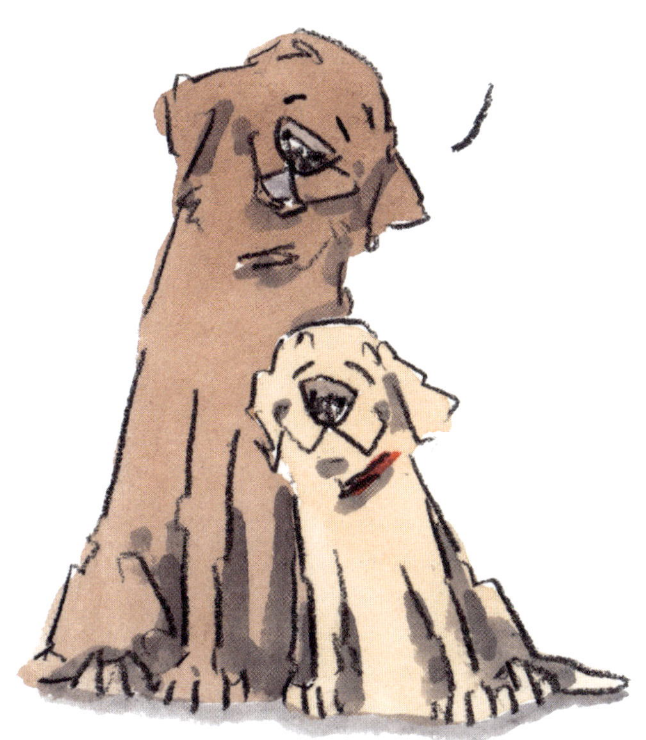

Sure, they could go
for a walk without us,
but it wouldn't be
anywhere near as much fun.

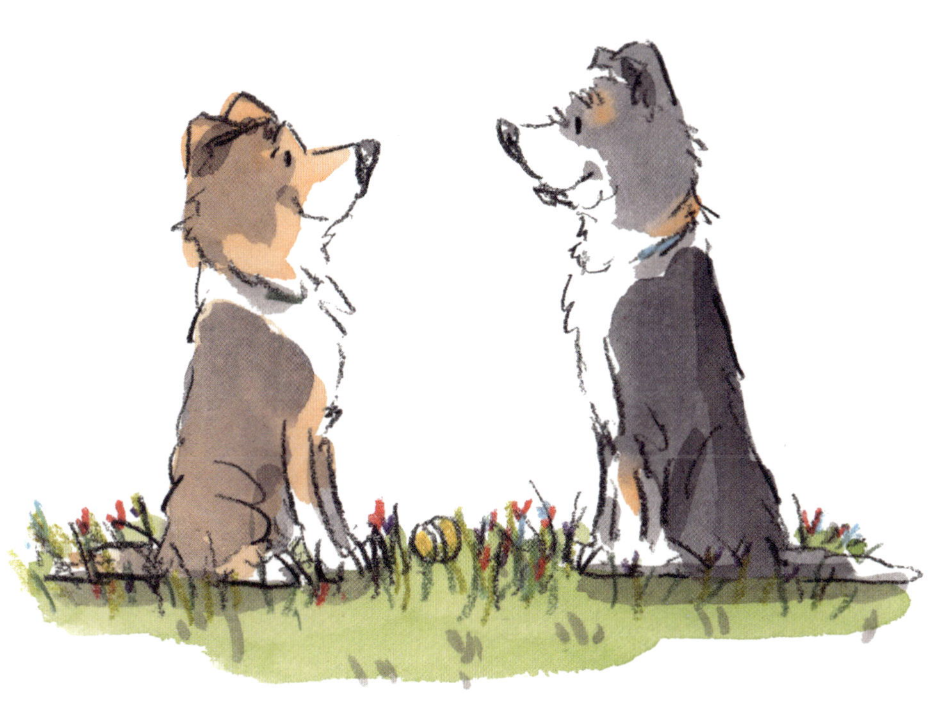

I am in air jail
for being
excessively
exuberant.

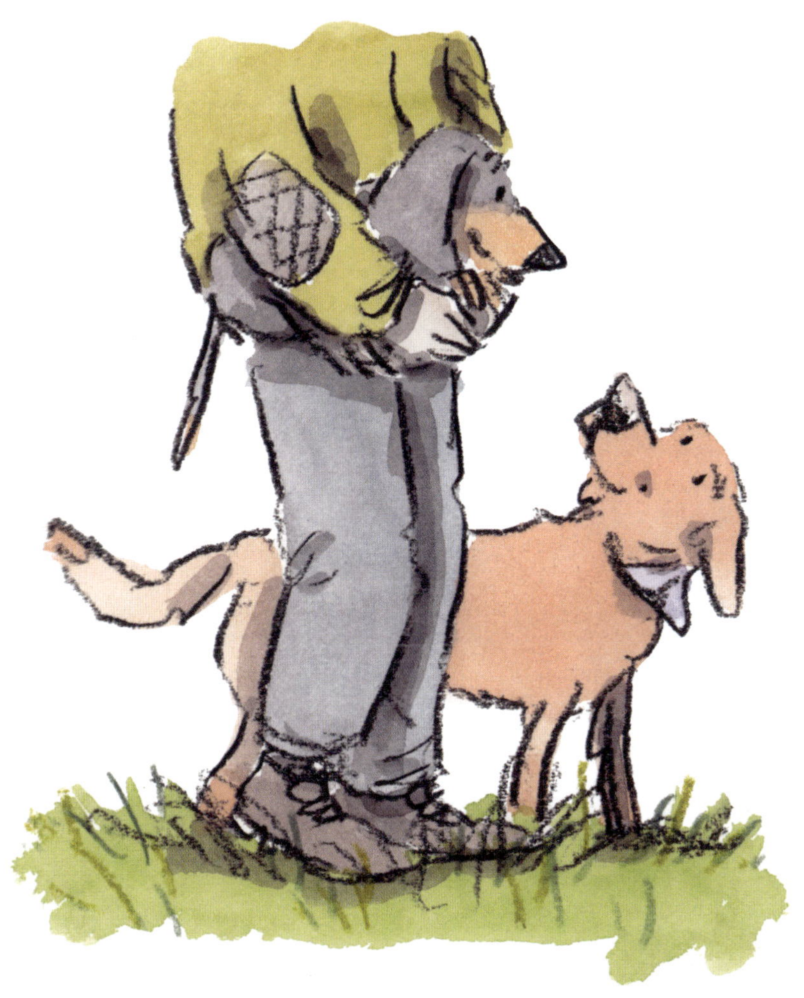

It is exhausting
being this
adorable.

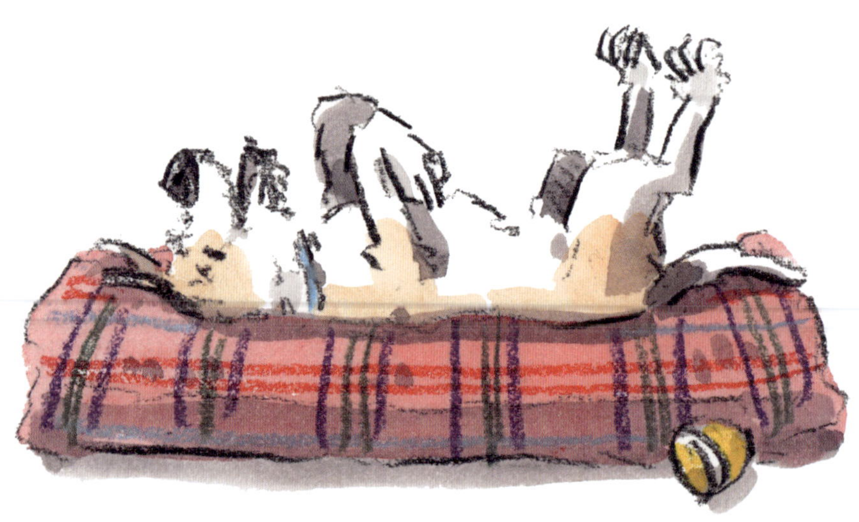

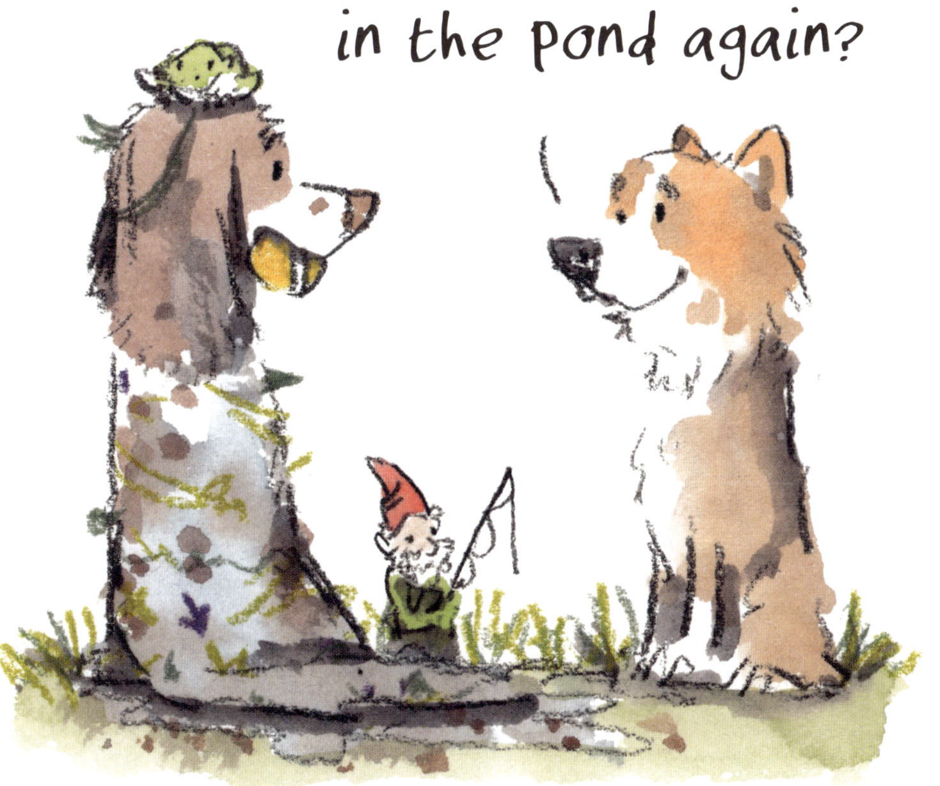

Did he throw the ball
in the pond again?

Home

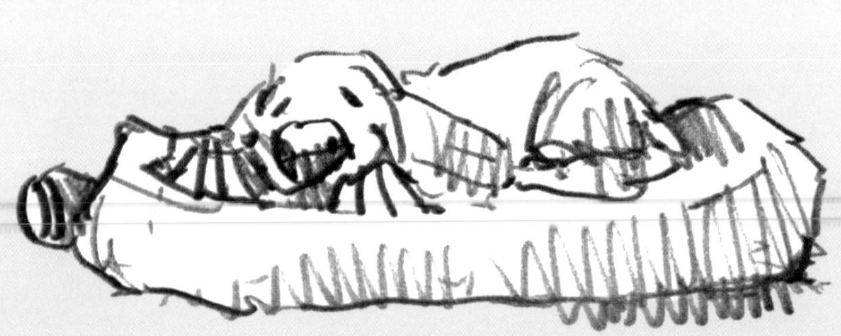

They are a whole minute
late with supper... this is
intolerable.

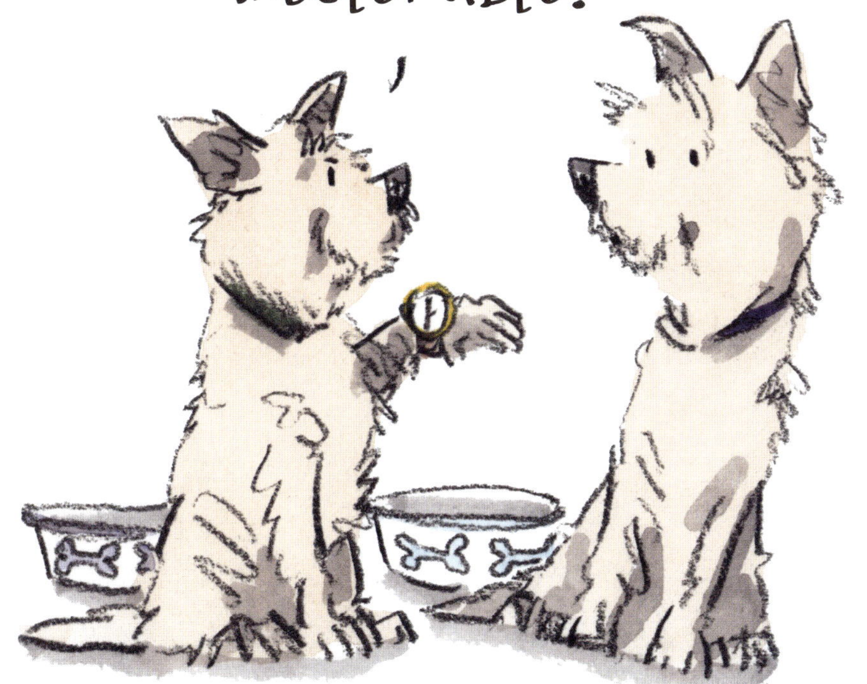

I'm the
welcoming committee.
If you haven't
got snacks,
you aren't coming in.

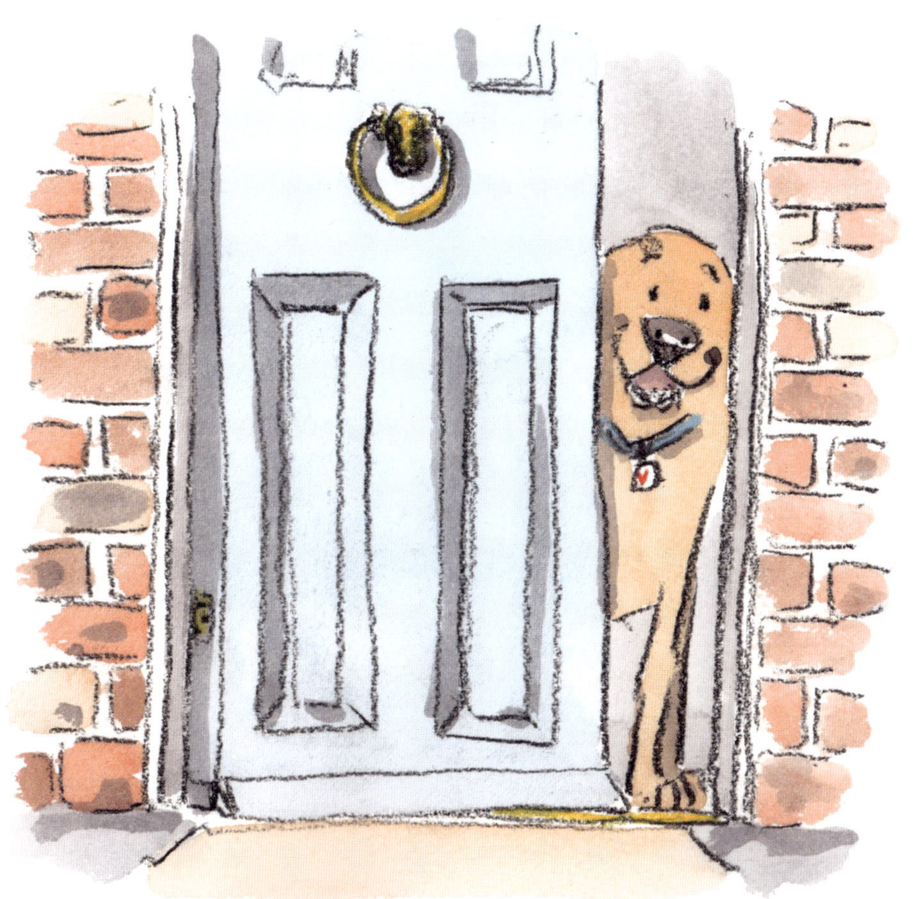

They think that being
this comfortable comes
easily to us, but it
actually takes years of
dedicated practice.

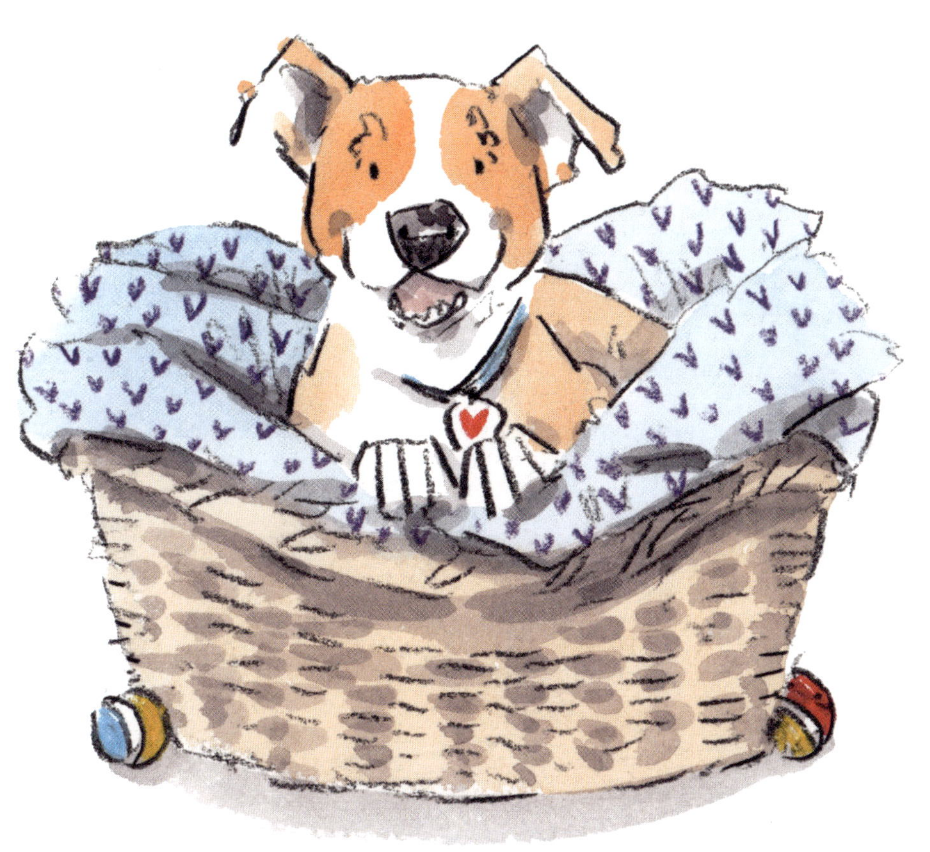

It may look like
I'm resting but I'm
actually on full alert.

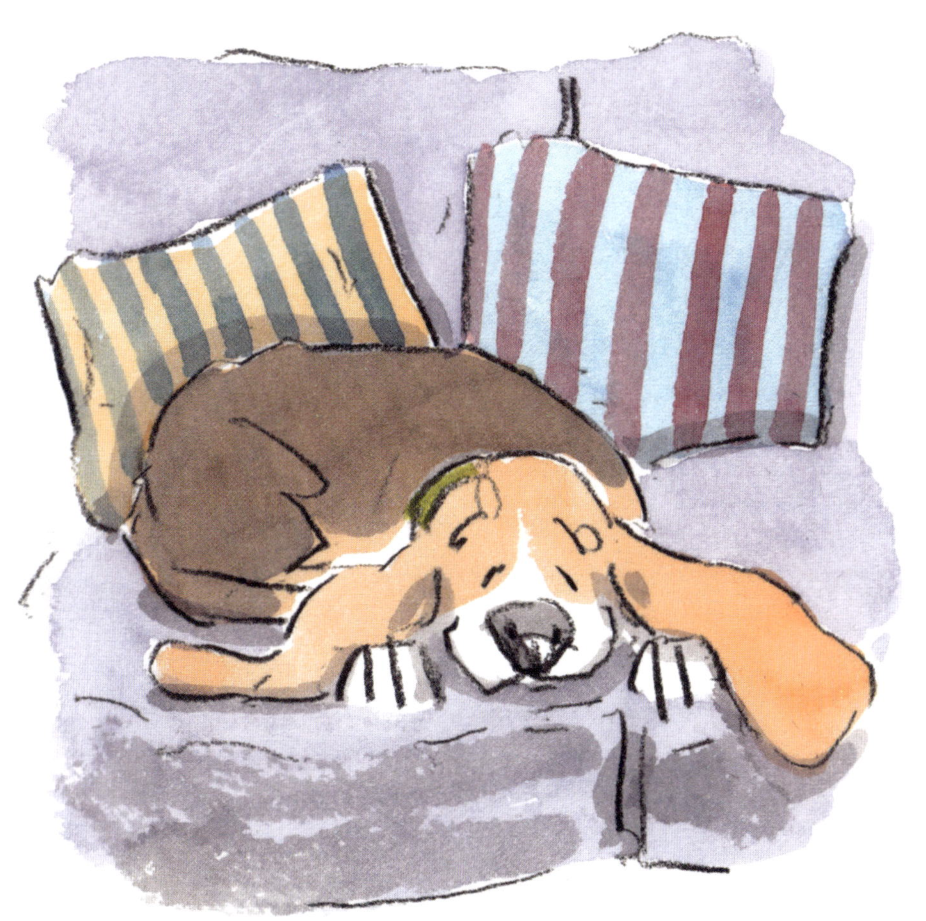

I could leap
into action at a
moment's notice.

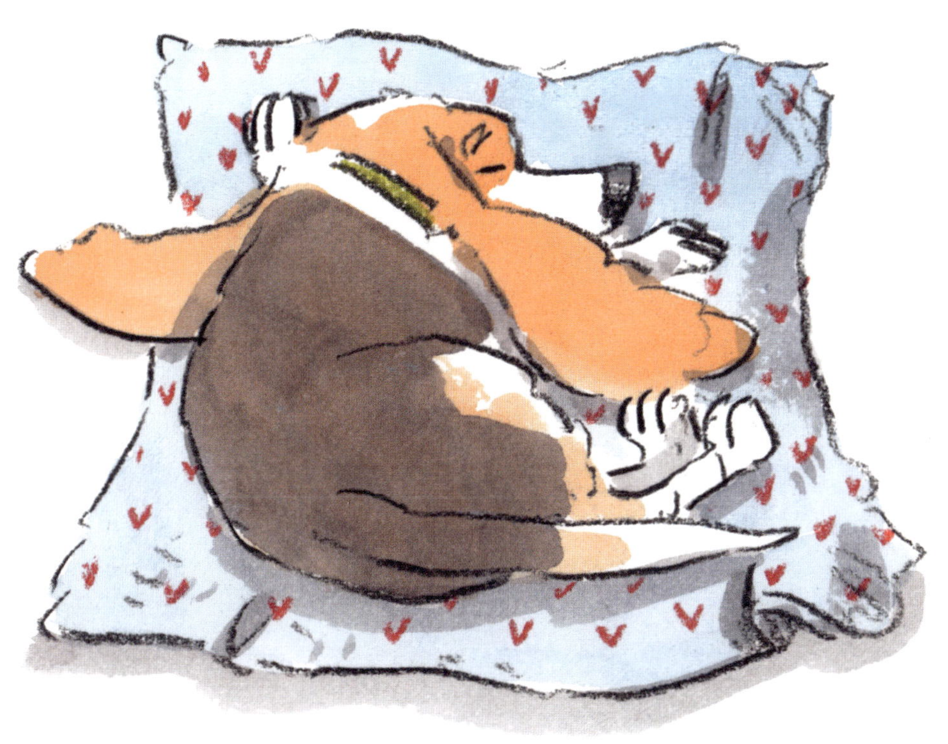

Everyone is safe
and sound with
me around.

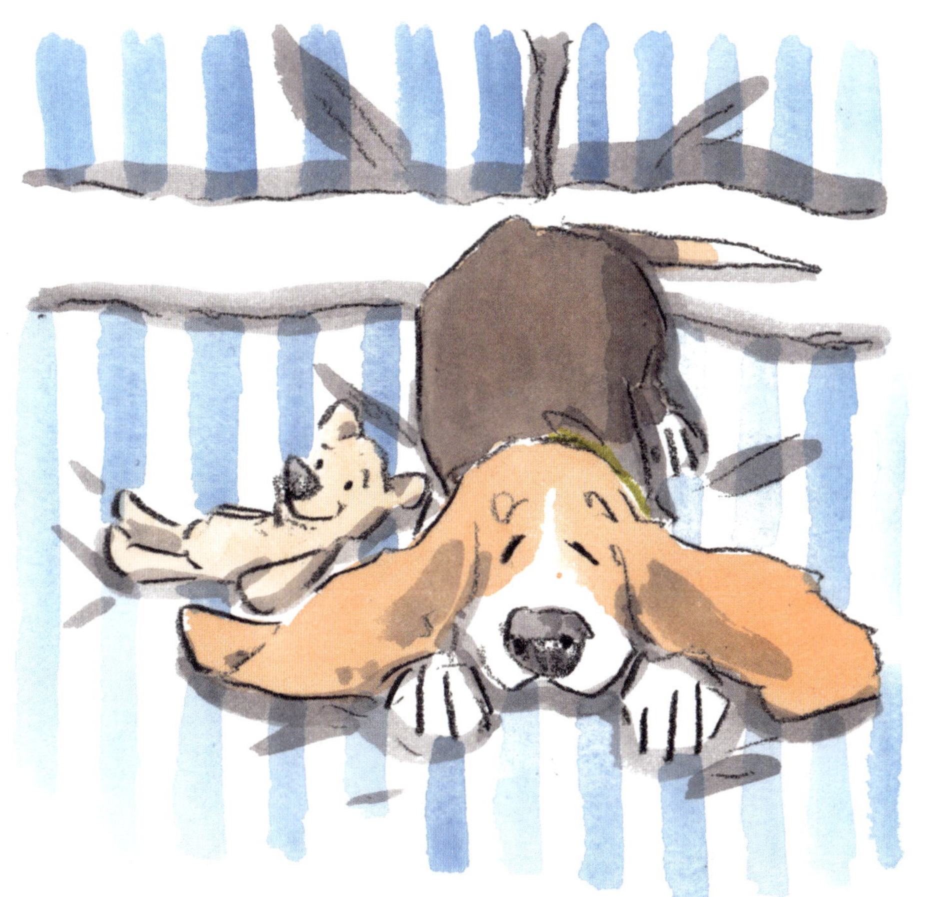

He keeps telling me not to shake in the house after a rainy walk, but...

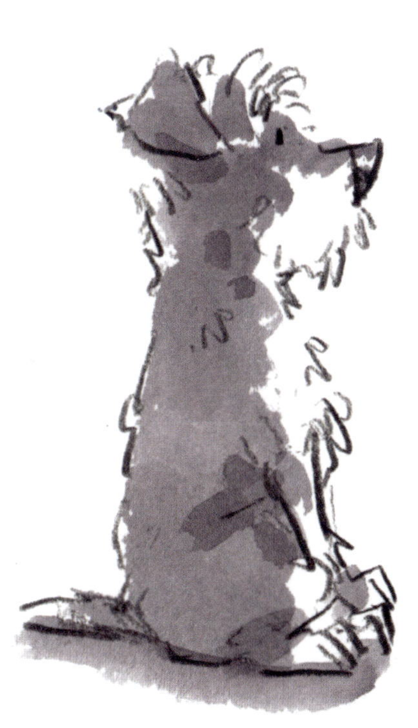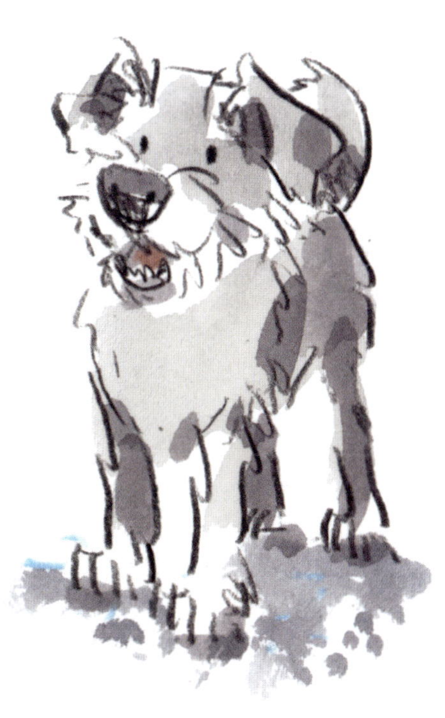

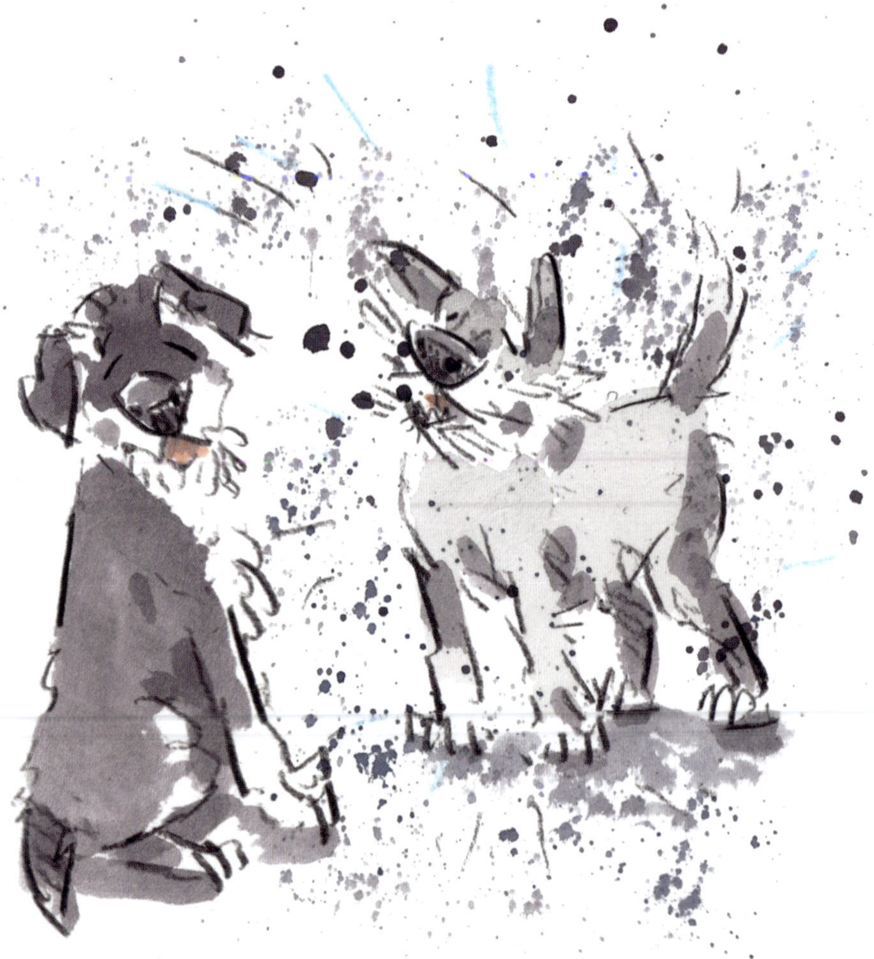

...a dog's got to do what
a dog's got to do.

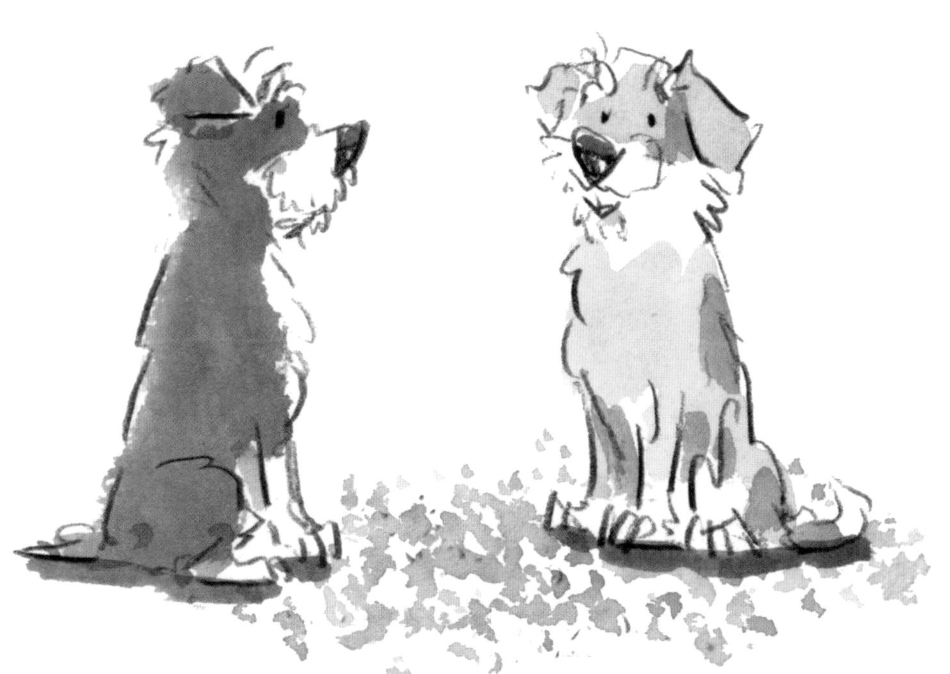

It looks a lot like
I'm relaxing, but I'm
actually hard at work
keeping your spot
warm for you.

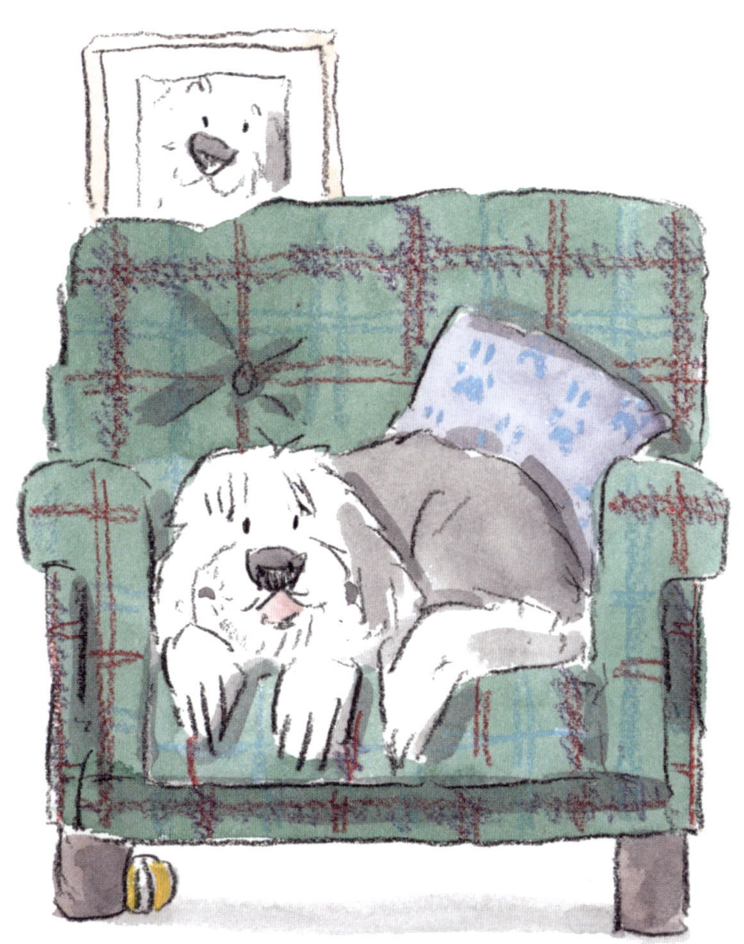

They have no idea
how long it is going to
take me to get good
and stinky again!!

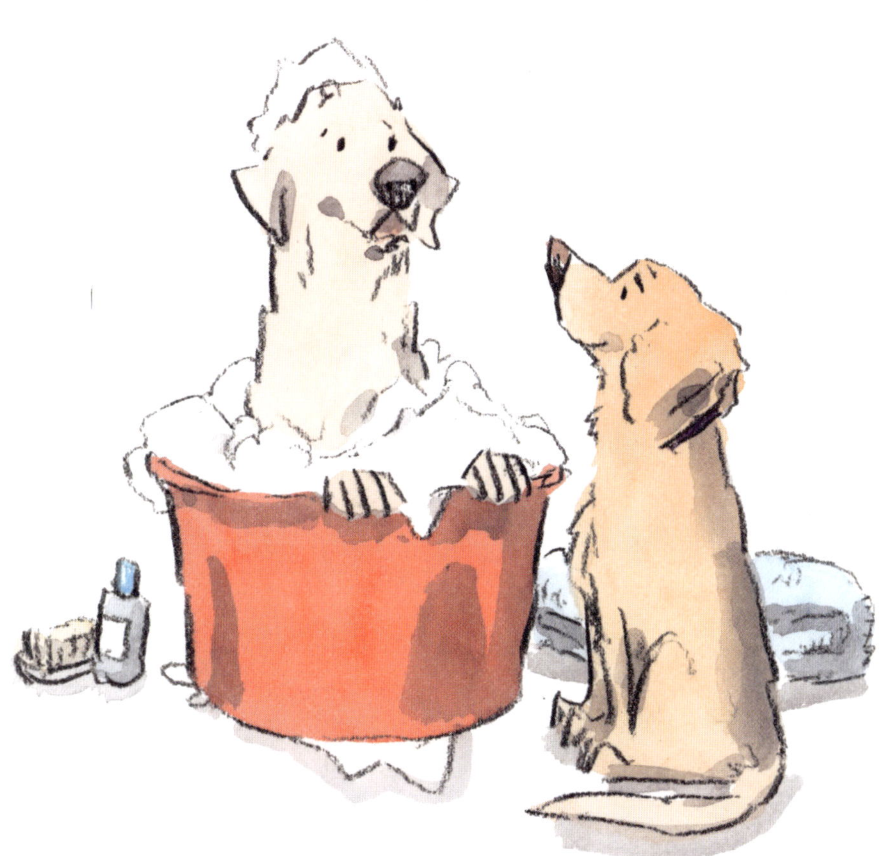

After hours of
exhaustive testing,
I declare this chair
comfortable.

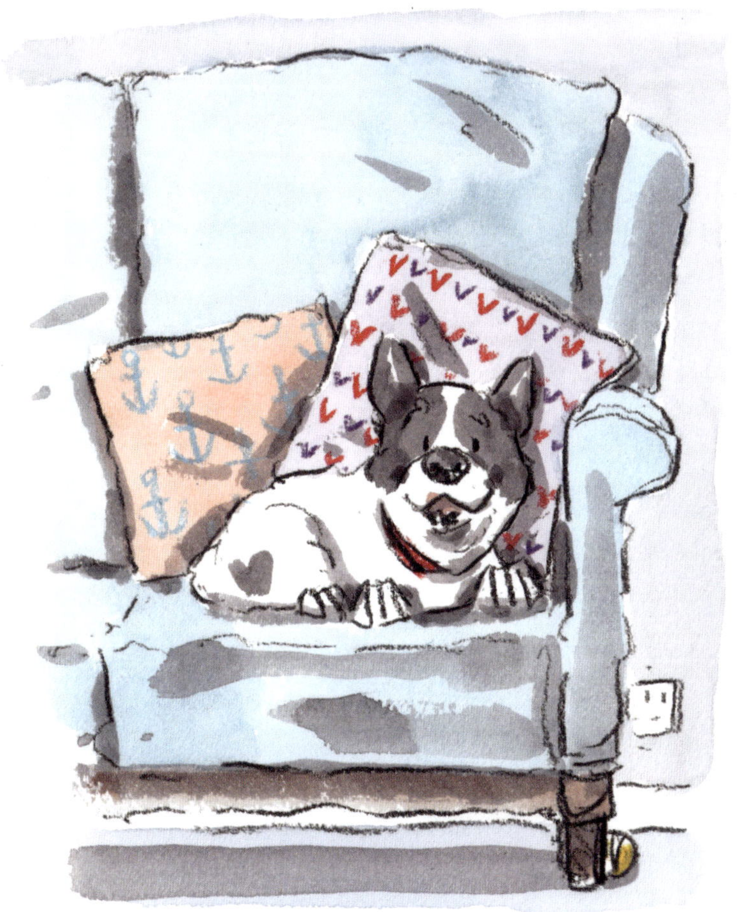

Just think, without us, they wouldn't know what time to get up in the morning.

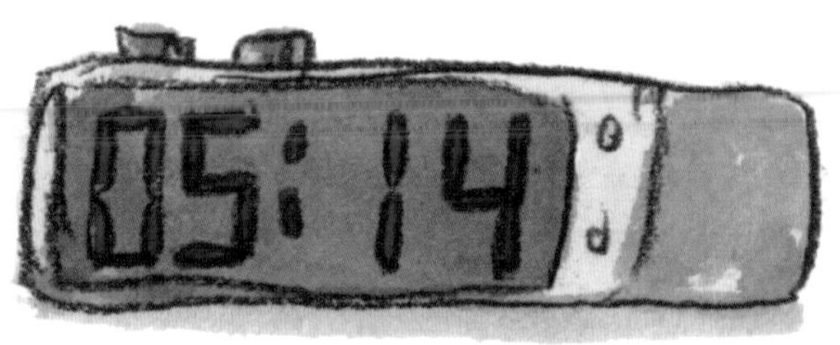

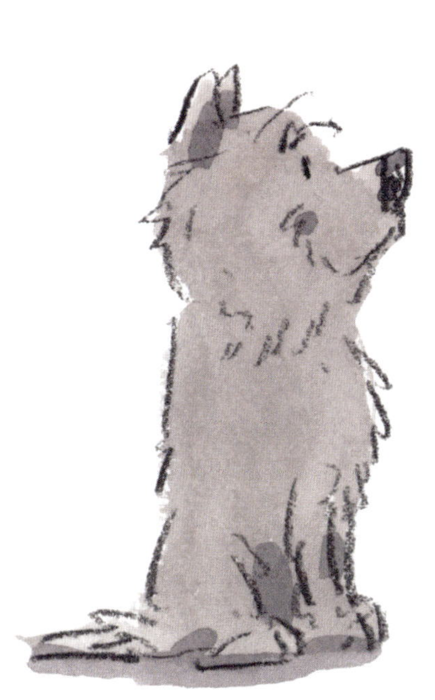
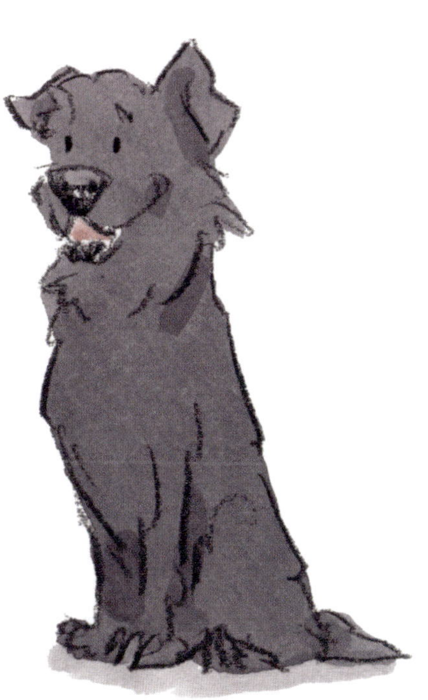

They would have
no idea when it was
time to eat.

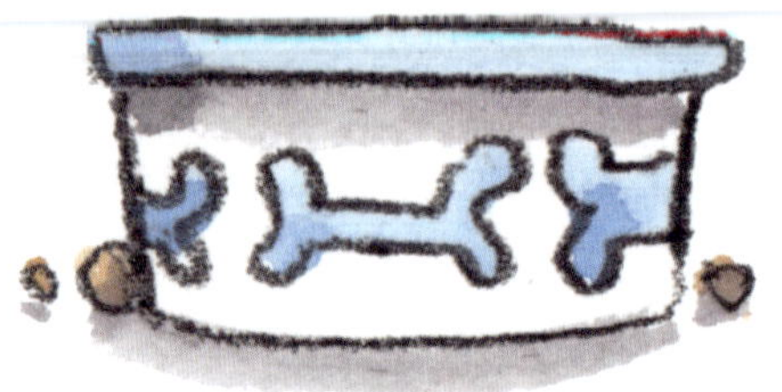

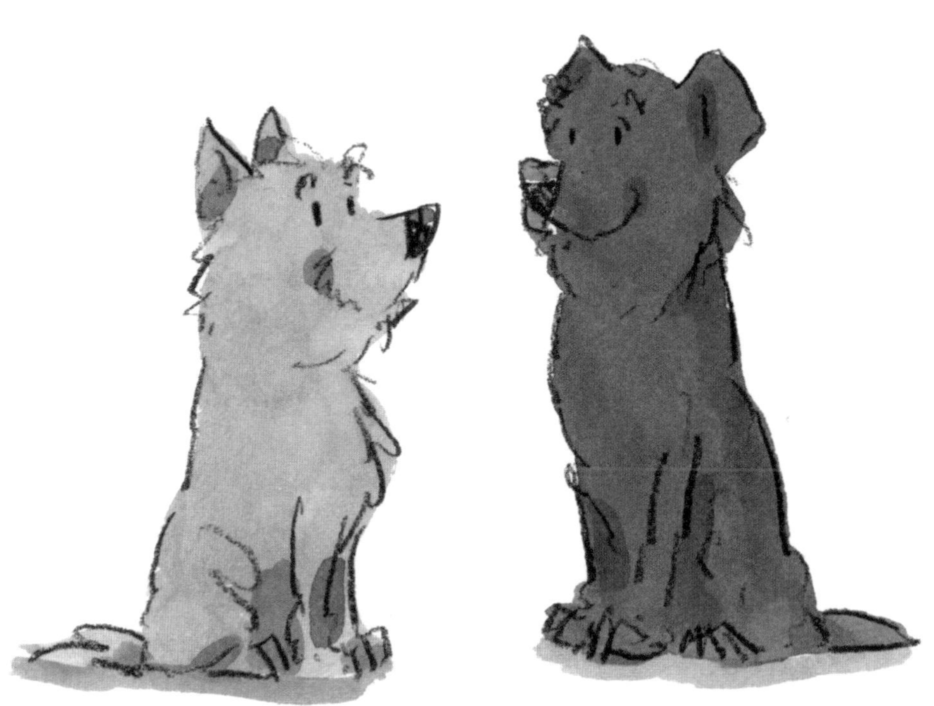

They wouldn't even
know when it was
Play time!!

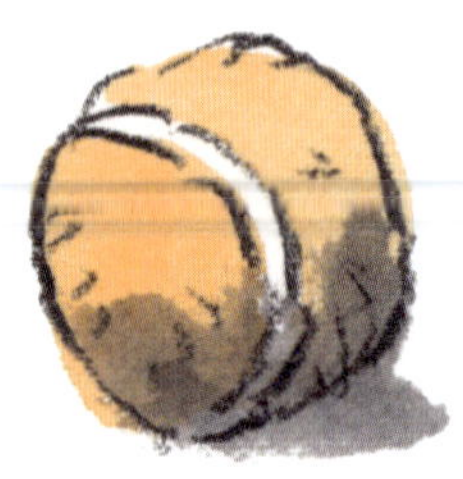

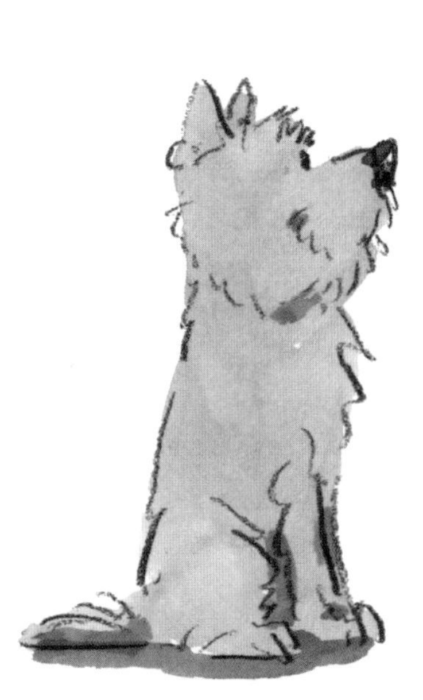
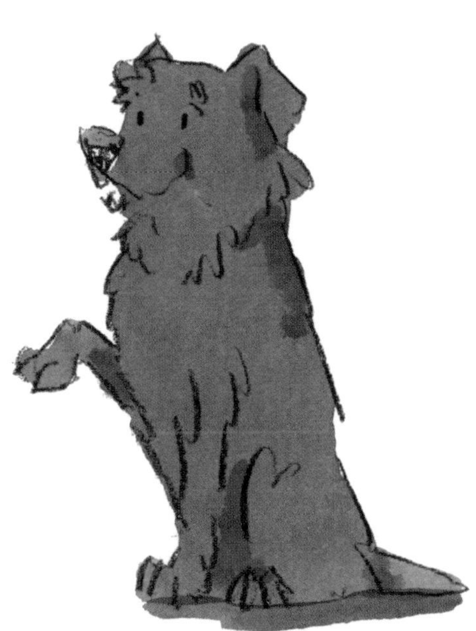

It's a good job
that we are here
to take care of them.

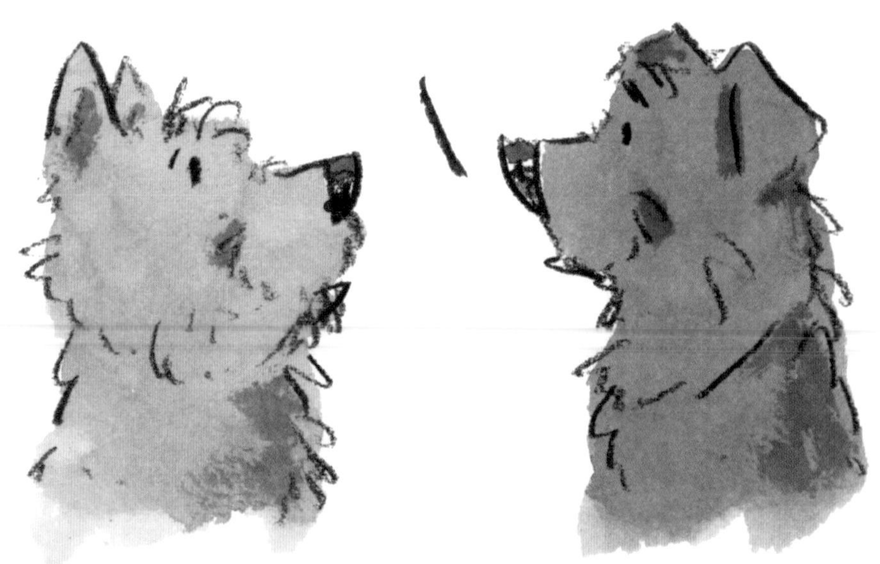

Love and Friendship

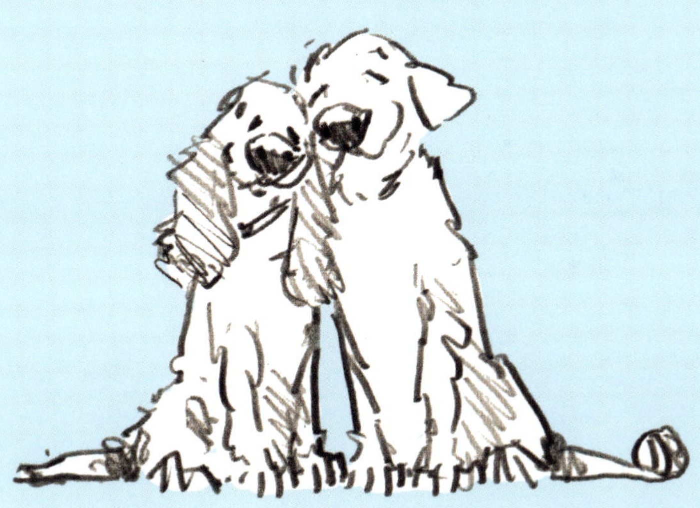

The thing
is, pup,

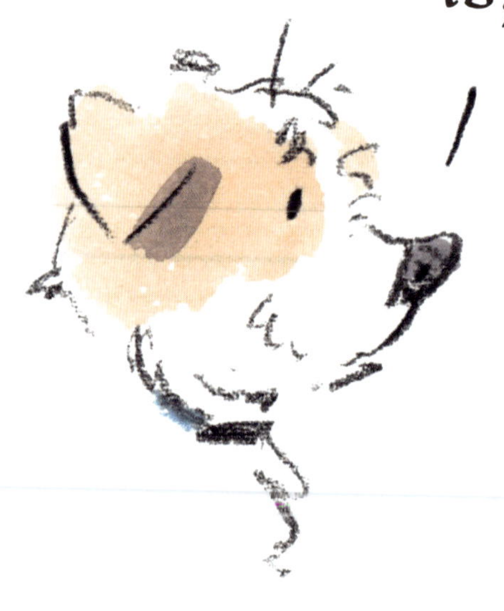

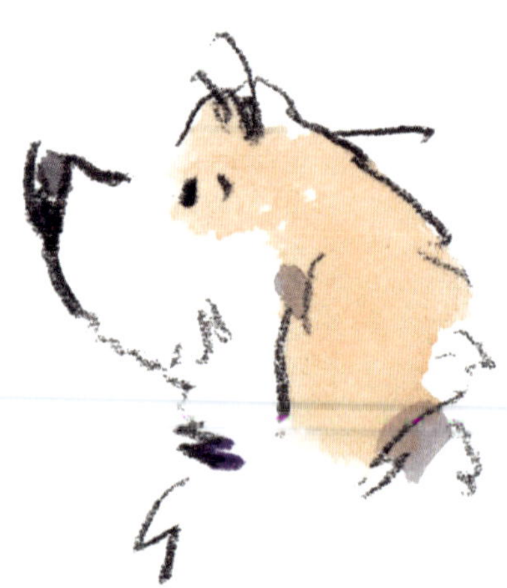

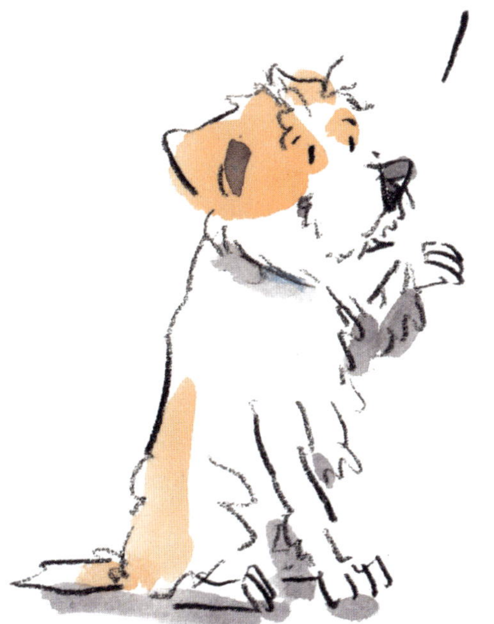
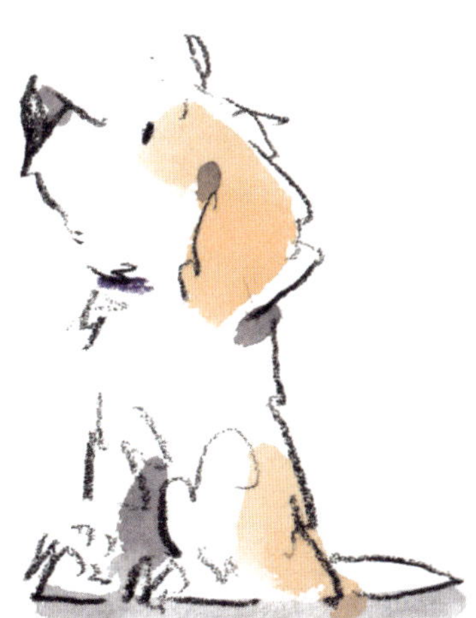

they don't
speak dog.

You can't just tell them
that you love them.
You have to show them,
every day.

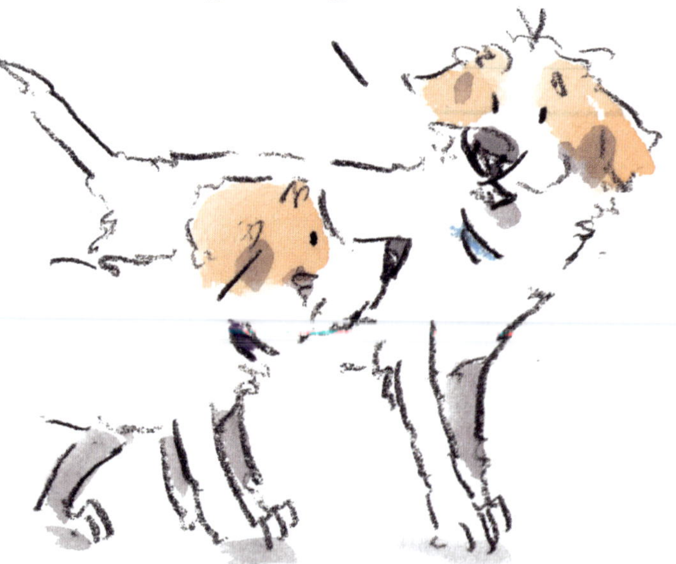

It's a lot of extra work
but I think that they are
worth it.

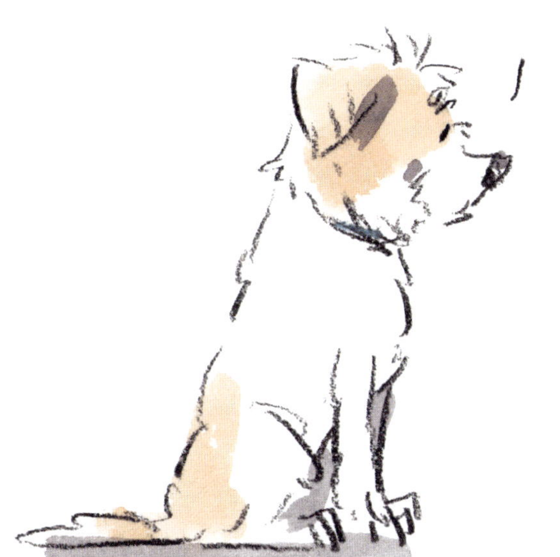

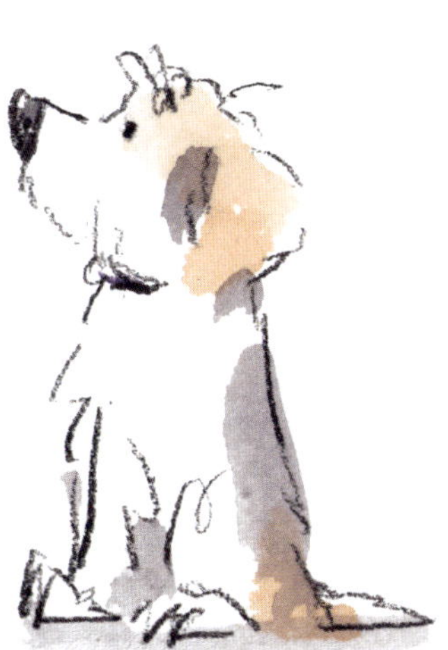

Being a dog is a
whatever the
weather...

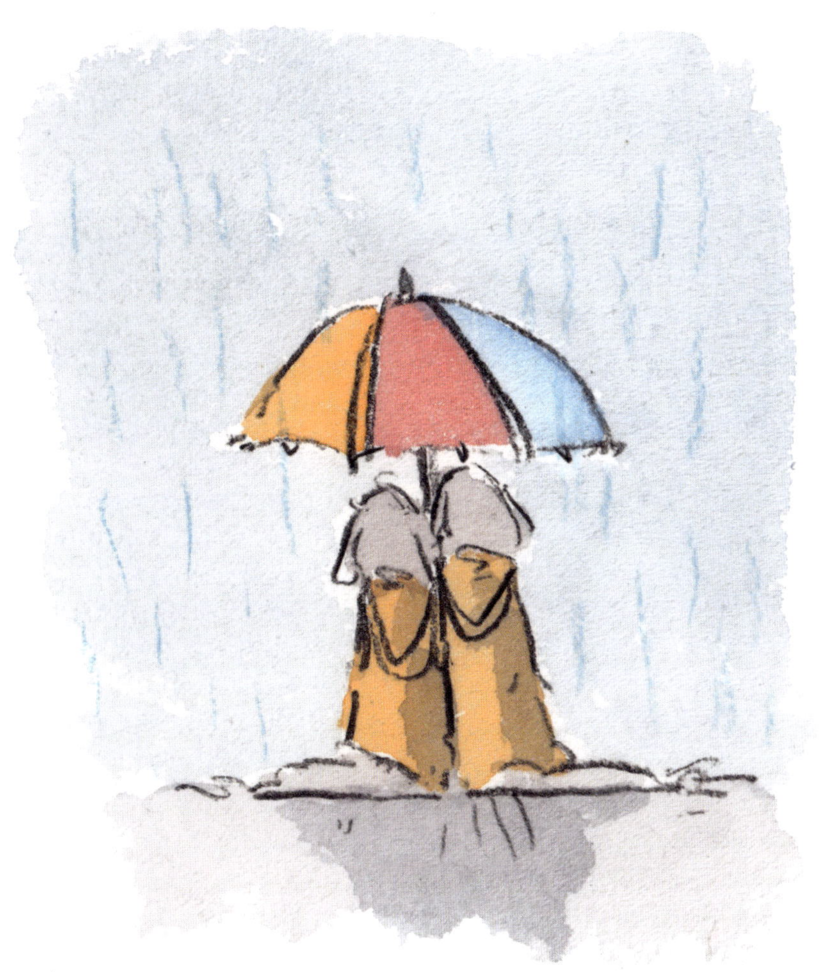

...from sunrise...

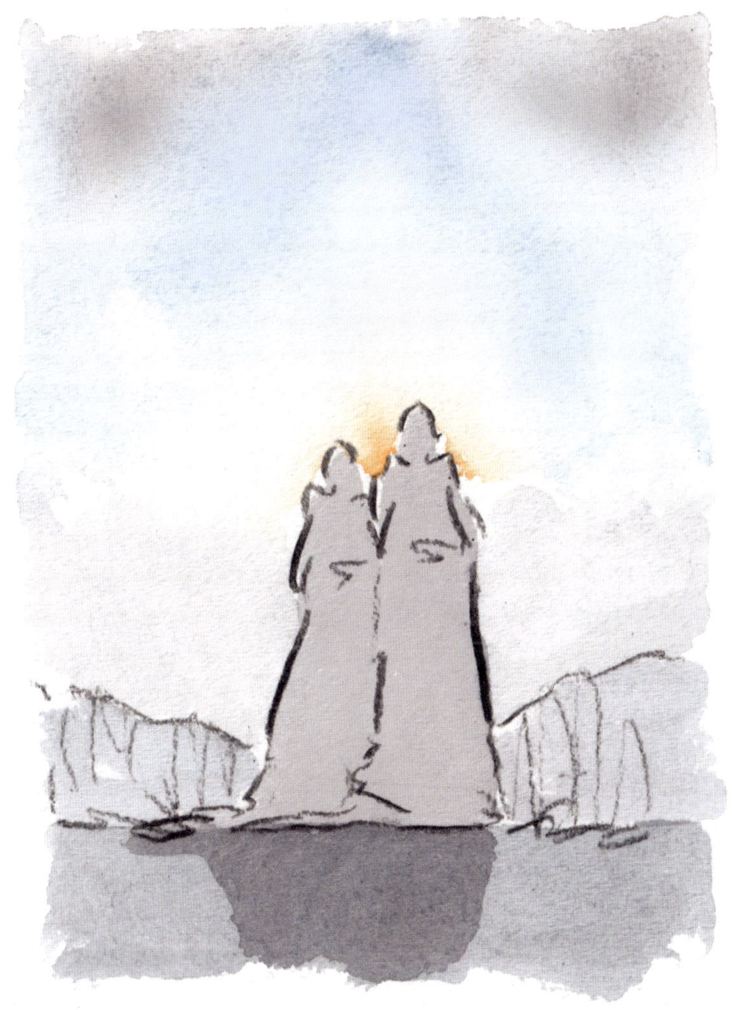

...to sunset...

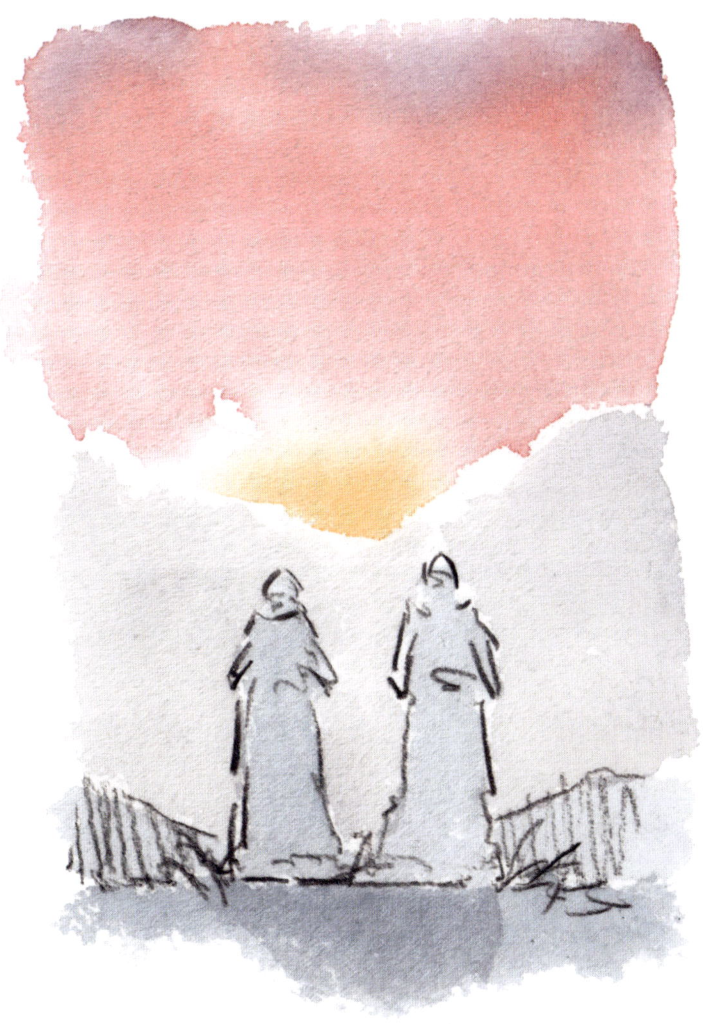

...till the stars
shine bright kind
of a job.

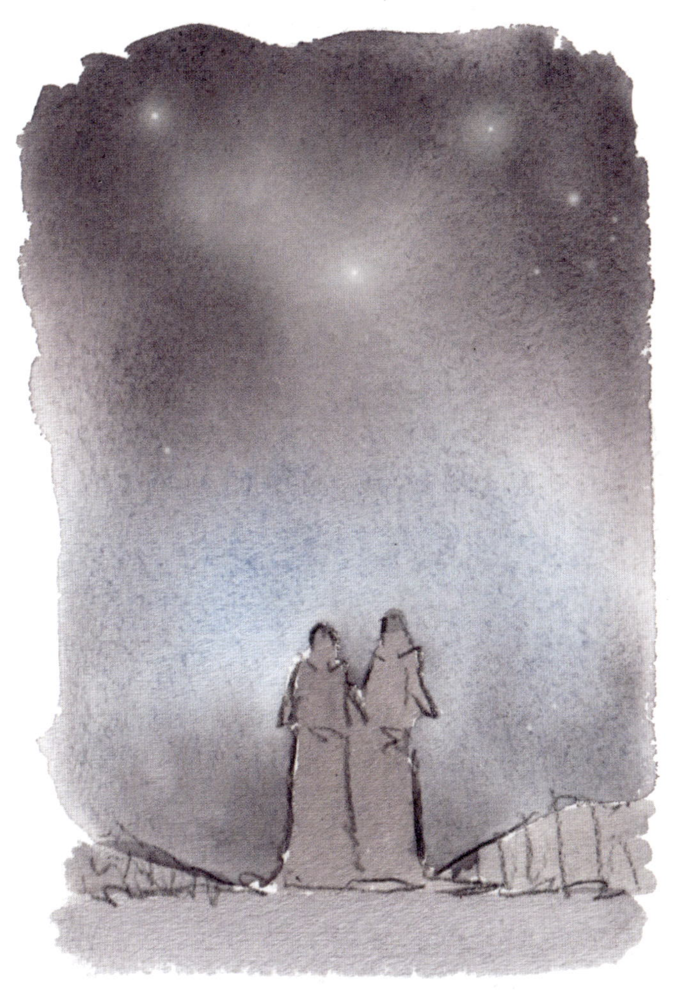

sniff

sniff

sniff

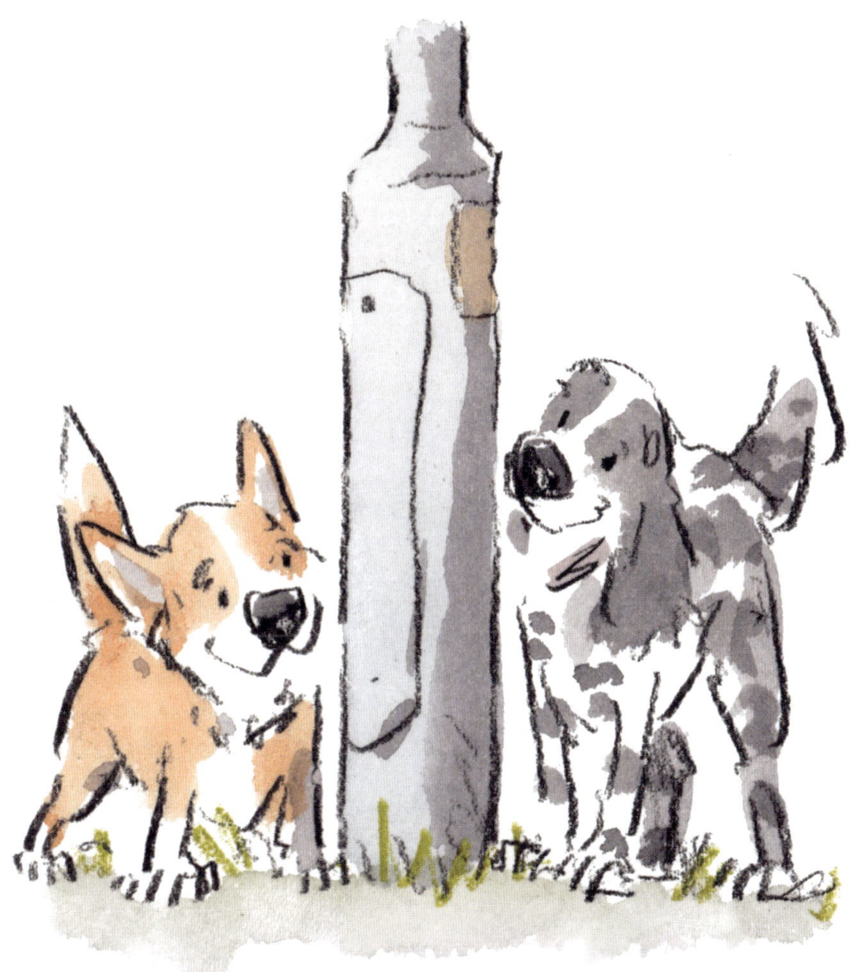

sniff

sniff

sniff

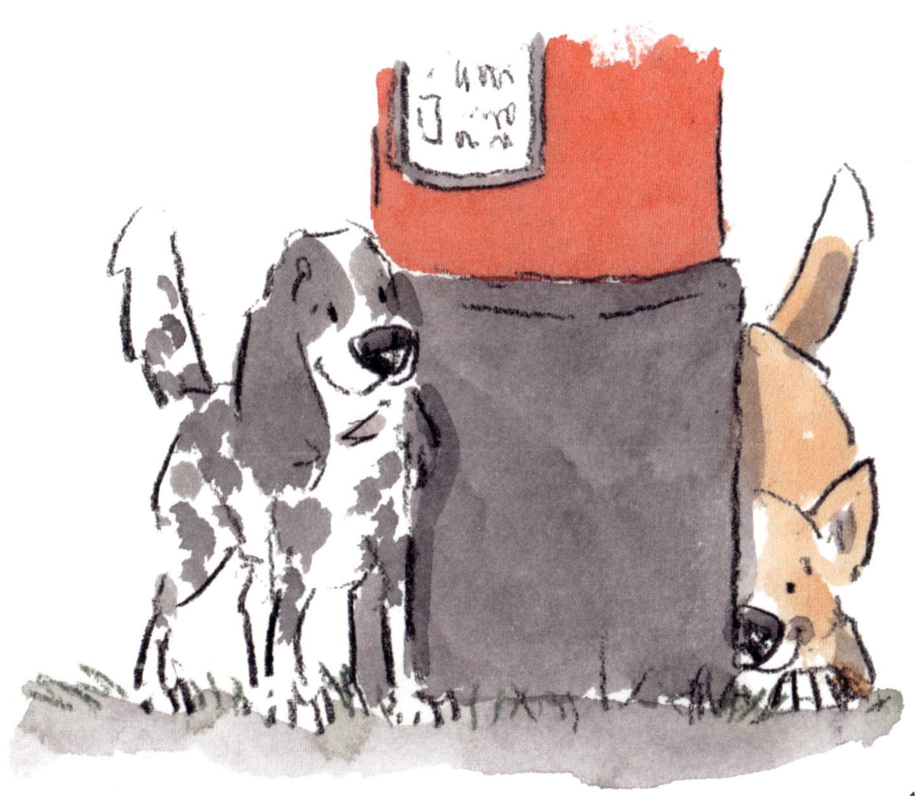

They have no idea
how much effort it
takes us to keep up
with our personal
correspondence.

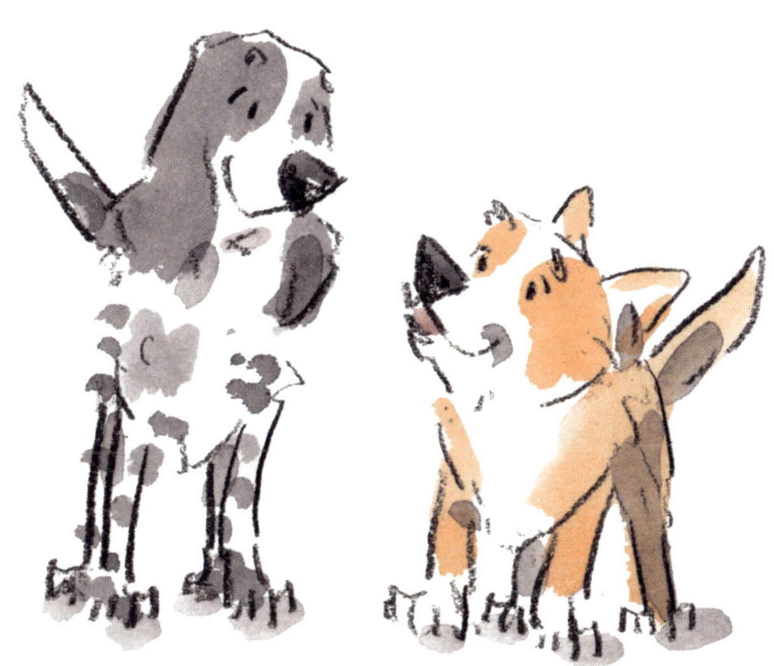

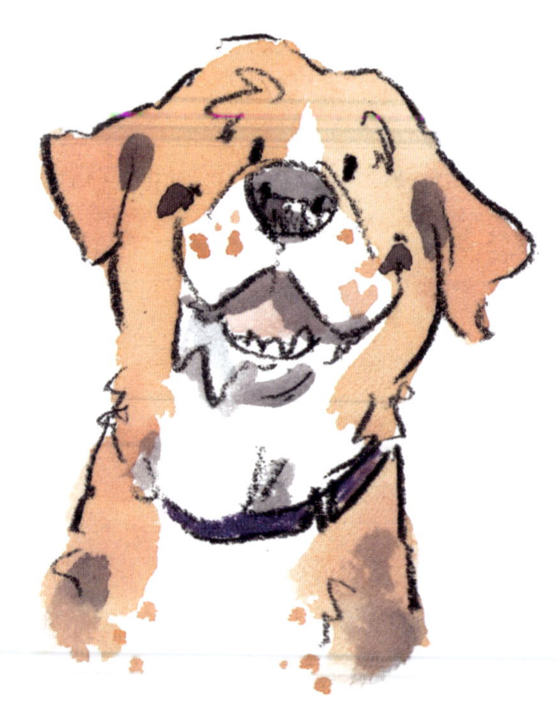

Slobber is my love language.

I'm her emotional
support terrier.

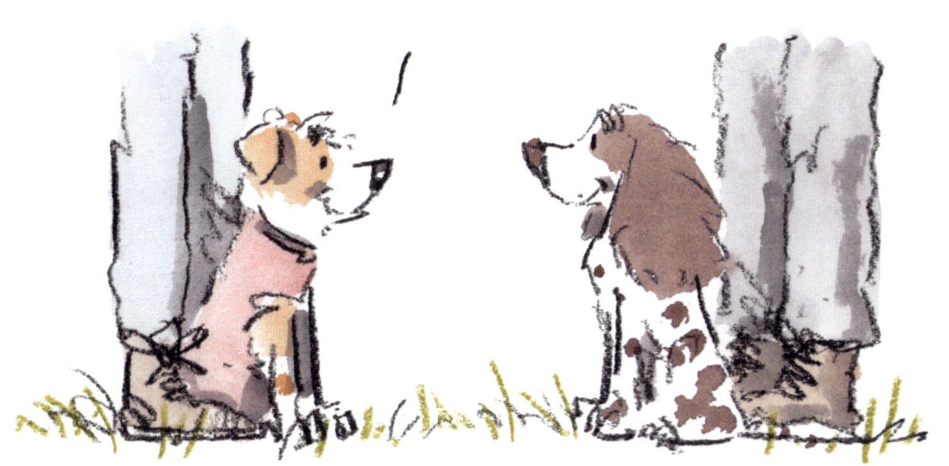

A large part of
being a dog, pup,
is being there for
our people.

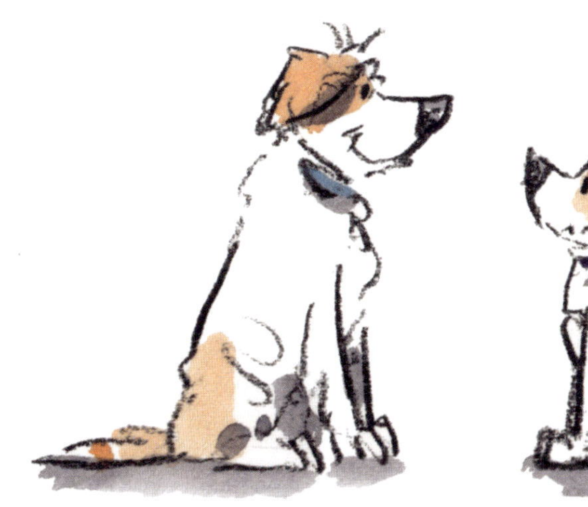
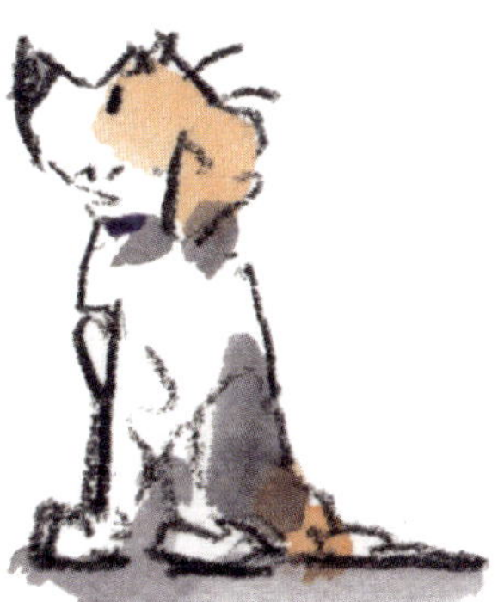

Being there when
she wants to talk,
to share the highs and
lows of her day.
We need to be there
to lend an ear.

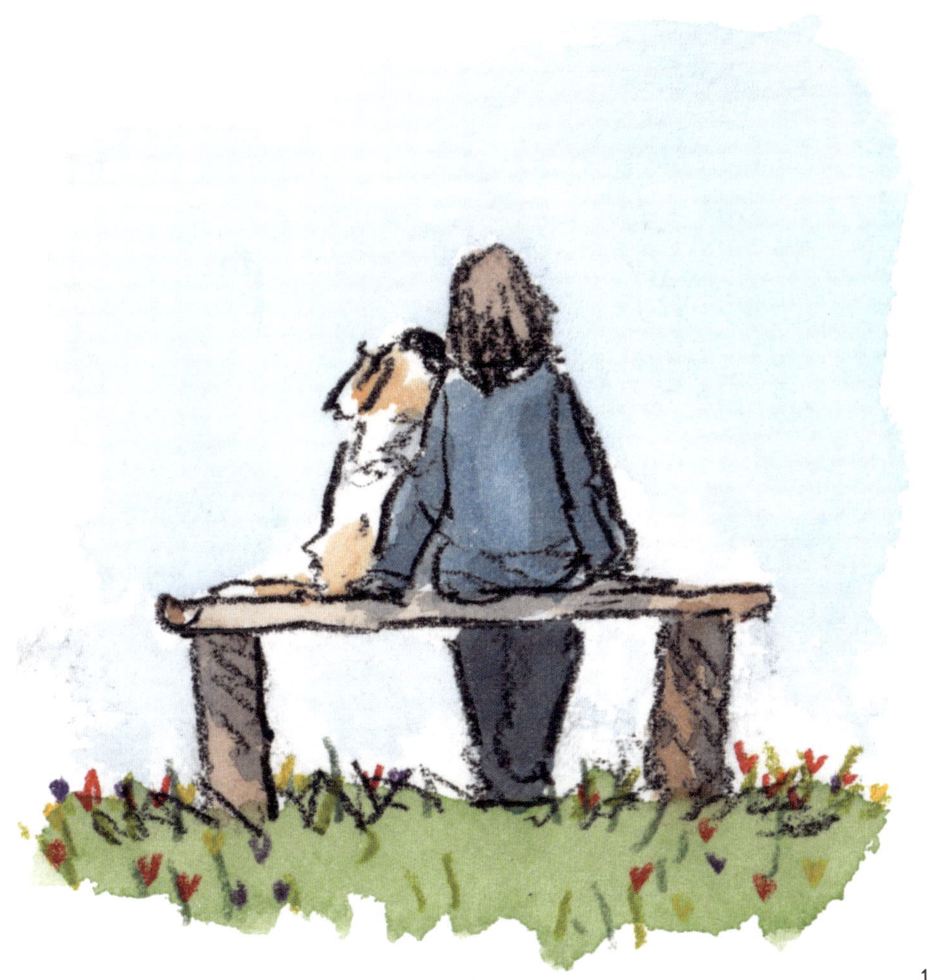

Sometimes she needs a friend to go on a walk with, to let the fresh air chase away her cares and fears, the worries she carries along the way.

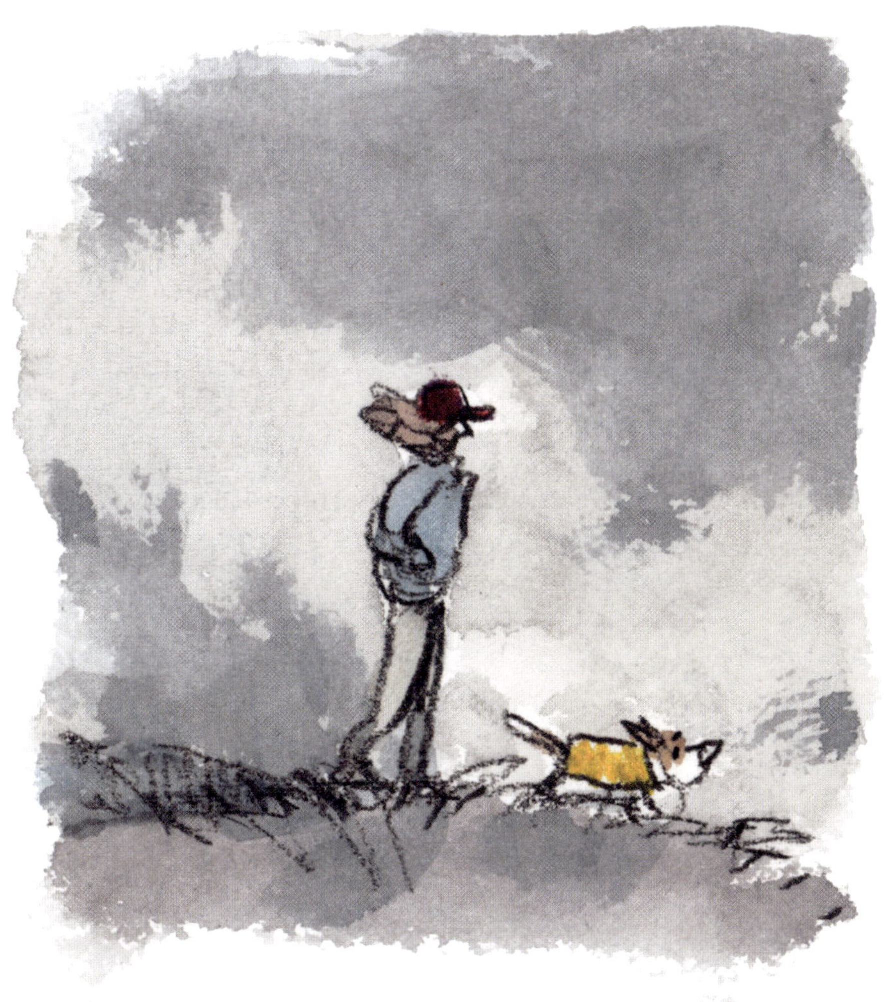

It's a tough job
being a dog,
isn't it?

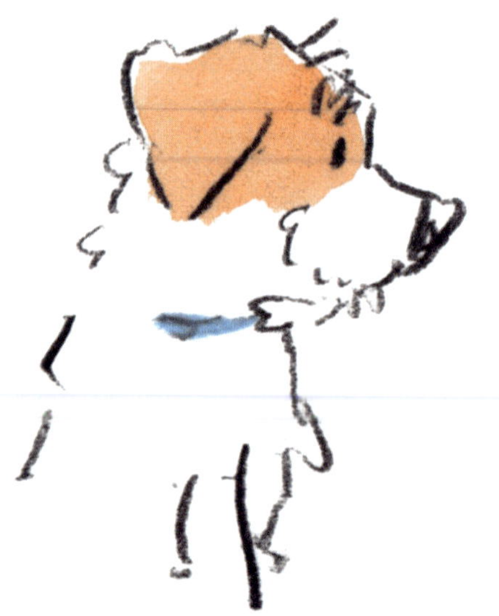

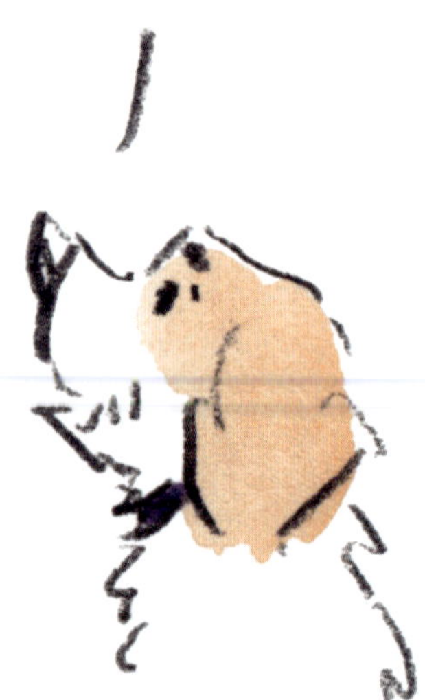

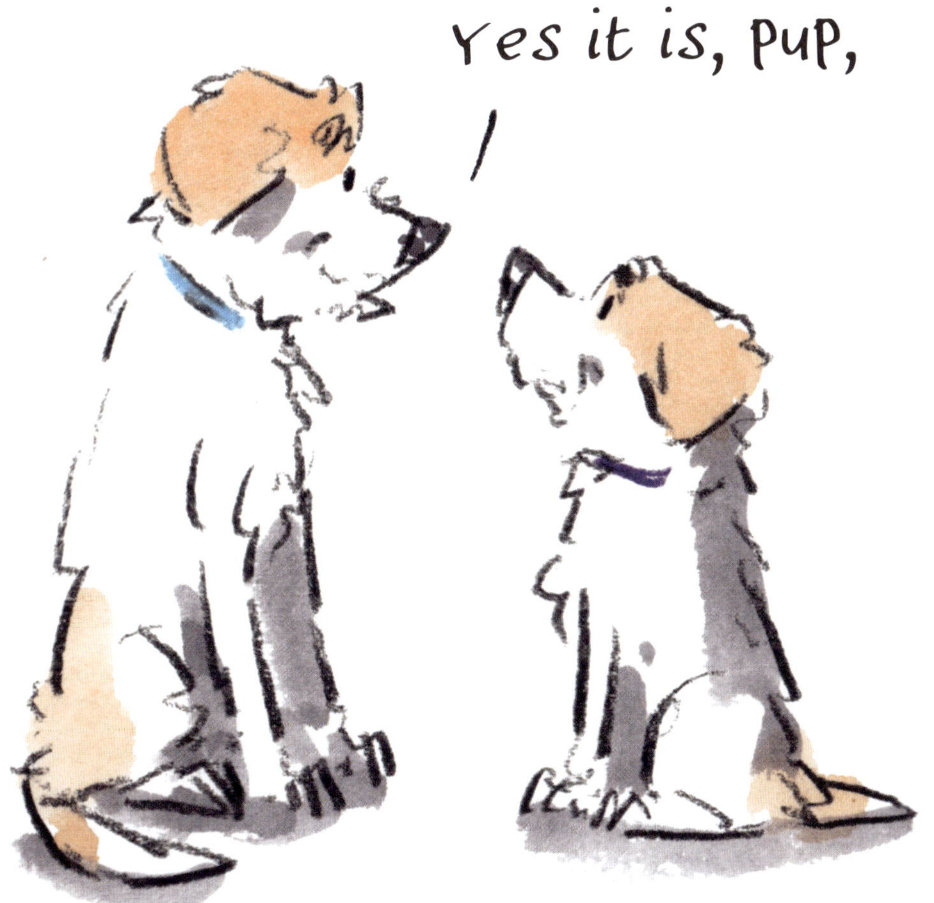

Yes it is, pup,

but I think that
you are going to be
really good at it.

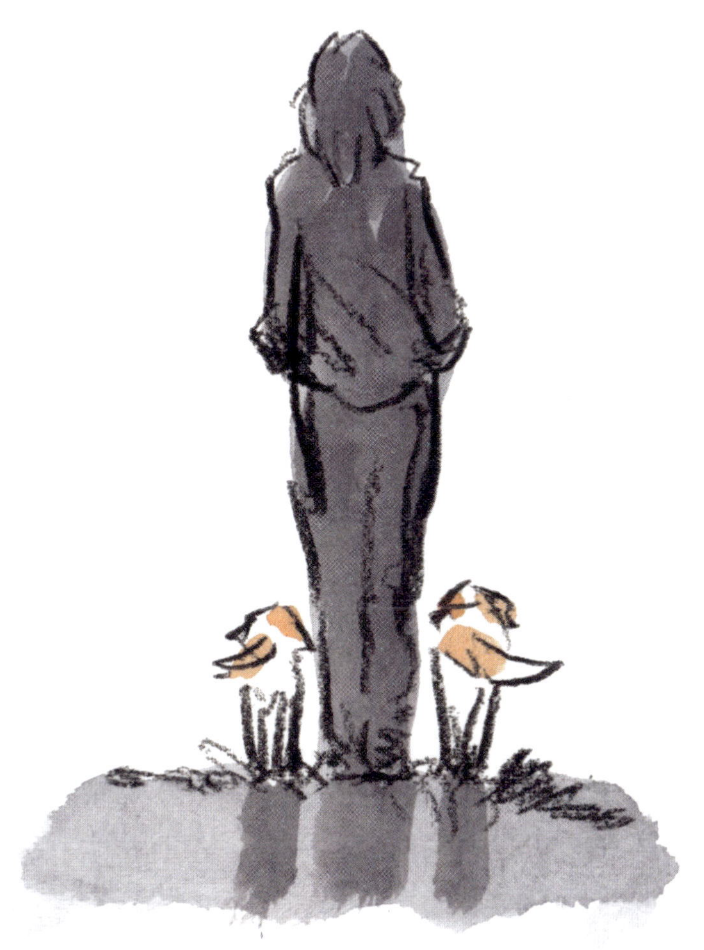

Acknowledgements

I wish to thank Dani Segelbaum, my agent, and her dog Dottie; Tom Asker, from HarperCollins, and his dog Murphy; Angharad, my wife, and our dogs Bella and Rab. I could not have made this book without their hard work, encouragement and inspiration.

I would also like to thank my Mum, Dad, Abs, David, Chris, Katherine and the boys, Rhiannon, Matthew and Daisy, Pat and Moss, Emma, Karen and Dave, Team Atkins, Reeko, Paul Olsewski, Bec Evans and all of my very lovely and dear friends who I talk to every day on social media about their wonderful dogs.

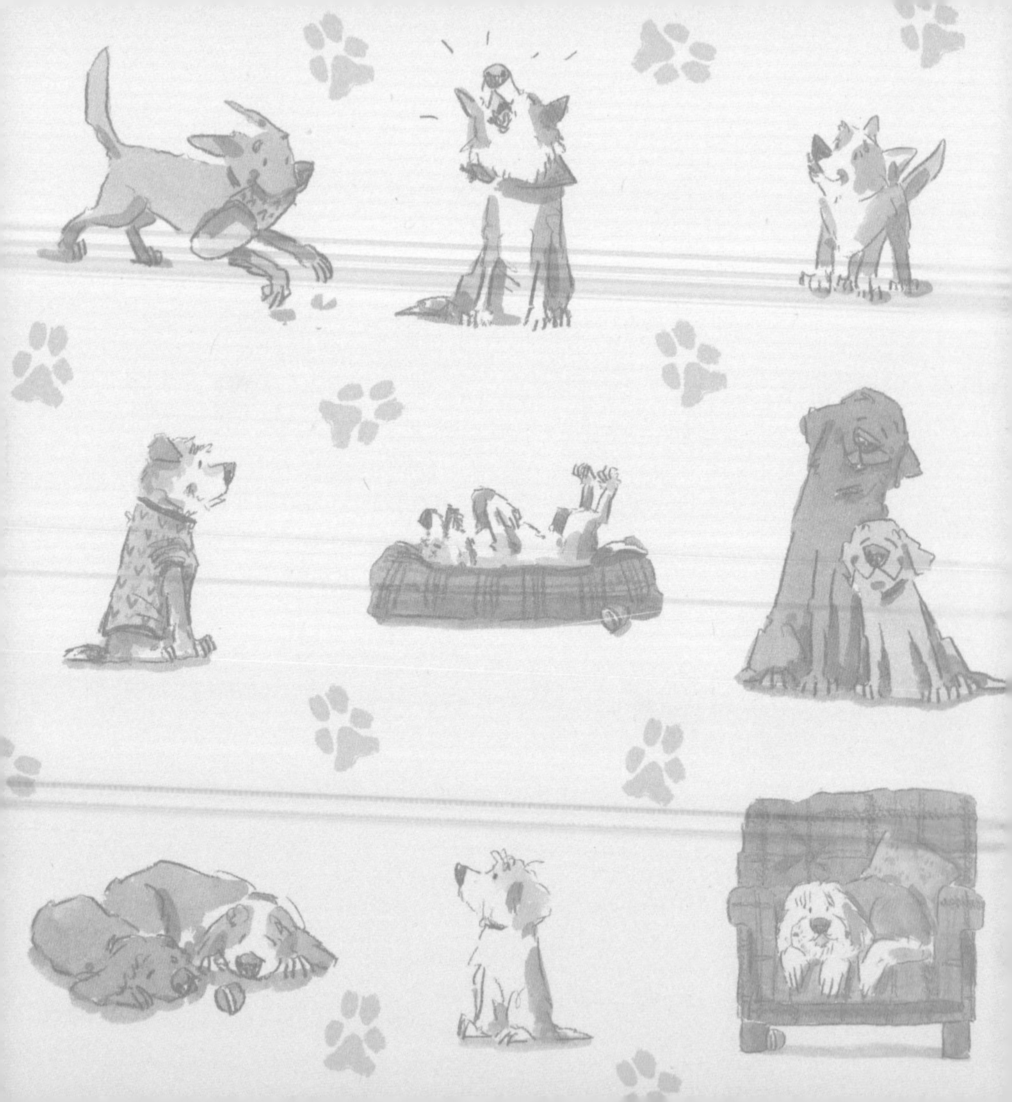